Advance Praise for *The Absolute Beginner's Guide to Cross-Examination*

"This is the book I wish I had when I started practicing law. An introduction to cross-examination, simplifying the most difficult skill a trial lawyer has to master. Each lesson is in a digestible short chapter easy to comprehend and the reader can put them right to work. And I love the examples Stern uses to illustrate the principles in action."
—Roy Black, Black Srebnick P.A.

"This punchy read makes it a pleasure to learn effective cross-examination techniques. Can't change the channel when you stumble across *My Cousin Vinny*? Stern masterfully utilizes it and other film trials to build your skills. This book shows that getting to great is easily as much fun as it is hard work."
—Justice John D. Couriel, Florida Supreme Court

"Through the entertaining use of three movie case studies, skilled trial lawyer and noteworthy teacher Sam Stern masterfully identifies and develops the key elements of and techniques for a successful cross-examination. Any trial lawyer who learns, implements, and practices the skills outlined in *The Absolute Beginner's Guide to Cross-Examination* will find cross-examination start to unfold at a slower pace, propelling the lawyer's ability to instantly recognize what's coming at them, and to effectively and persuasively react."
—Michael Critchley Sr., Critchley, Kinum, and Luria LLC

"*The Absolute Beginner's Guide to Cross-Examination* is a master class on cross-examination. Using a rich assortment of vignettes and aphorisms, Stern takes the reader through a clinic on the principles of how to handle an adverse witness. Then weaving in trials from movies, he puts the lessons into context to show how they were effective or ineffective. This book is a must-read for litigators and should be studied by anyone looking to begin or those looking to take their trial skills to an advanced level."

—Roscoe C. Howard Jr., former United States Attorney, District of Columbia, Barnes & Thornburg LLP

"Many of us learned what we know about trying cases 'at the knee' of Judge Herbert J. Stern, whose groundbreaking work *Trying Cases to Win* changed the course of our careers. The torch now passes to the next generation with this exciting book which demonstrates that no one understands the techniques of cross-examination better than Sam Stern. He is a gifted teacher as well as a formidable trial advocate."

—Harry L. Manion III, Hunton Andrews Kurth LLP

"Sam Stern makes cross-examination—which is so stressful for lawyers—accessible and fun. There's a lot to learn here for beginners and even for veteran trial lawyers."

—David O. Markus, Markus Moss PLLC, creator of the *SDFL Blog* and *For the Defense* podcast

"Sam Stern's book provides a creative roadmap and invaluable guide to the challenges posed by cross-examination. He masterfully uses case studies based on popular trial-related movies to demonstrate effective cross-examination as well as where important opportunities are missed. The book reminds beginning as well as seasoned trial lawyers of the importance of using cross-examination to develop the theory of your case, while at the same time maintaining credibility as an advocate."

—Jon A. Sale, former Assistant Special Watergate Prosecutor, Nelson Mullins LLP

The Absolute Beginner's Guide to
CROSS-EXAMINATION

The Absolute
Beginner's Guide to
CROSS-EXAMINATION

SAMUEL A. STERN

Skyhorse Publishing

Skyhorse Publishing books may be purchased in bulk at special discounts for sales promotion, corporate gifts, fund-raising, or educational purposes. Special editions can also be created to specifications. For details, contact the Special Sales Department, Skyhorse Publishing, 307 West 36th Street, 11th Floor, New York, NY 10018 or info@skyhorsepublishing.com.

Skyhorse® and Skyhorse Publishing® are registered trademarks of Skyhorse Publishing, Inc.®, a Delaware corporation.

Visit our website at www.skyhorsepublishing.com.

10 9 8 7 6 5 4 3 2 1

Library of Congress Cataloging-in-Publication Data is available on file.

Cover design by Kai Texel
Cover image provided by Stern LLC

Print ISBN: 978–1-5107–6885-7
Ebook ISBN: 978–1-5107–6886-4

Printed in the United States of America

To my family

Contents

PART 2

Acknowledgments

We all stand on the shoulders of those who came before us. I was incredibly fortunate to be taught by Herbert J. Stern, one of the great trial lawyers and teachers. I say that, not as a biased son, but as a professional exposed to a range of ideas on the subject. The biography *Tiger in the Court* inspired me to become a lawyer, and his *Trying Cases to Win* books and in-person seminars developed my skills. I am far from alone in this experience, as countless other lawyers have been shaped by him as well. The profession and the public are fortunate to have him and those like him who strive to leave things better than they found them.

I also wish to acknowledge the University of Virginia School of Law Trial Advocacy College and its incredible faculty. Having been there most of my life, first as an observer, then as a student, and now as a member of the faculty, it has significantly impacted my personal and professional development. While I regret omitting anyone from its celebrated faculty, I would be remiss not to specifically mention Thomas Campion, Stephen Duncan, Stephen Farmer, Barry Fredericks, Charles Gorham, and Gerald Ivey as outstanding trial lawyers and teachers from whom I have learned a great deal.

My thanks to the University of Miami School of Law for giving me the opportunity to teach there. I firmly xiv The Absolute Beginner's Guide to Cross-Examination

believe we can always be better at what we do. When we learn how to effectively teach others, we don't just give back, we push ourselves to new places.

I also wish to thank all of the attorneys I have worked with as well as my adversaries over the years. When we are challenged by talented people, we find that we are capable of more than we thought.

Preface

The journey of a thousand miles begins with one step.
　　　　　　　　　　　　　　　　　　—Lao Tzu

O ur first step is to understand why effective cross-examination is important. Whenever we appear before a trier of fact on behalf of a client, we assume an awesome responsibility. To the client, the case may impact any number of factors, from their finances to their reputations, and even their liberty. Representing those interests is an honor, of course, but it is also a daunting responsibility because there will be a lawyer on the other side doing their best to present a different version of the "truth." One of the ways that these competing "truths" will be tested is through the cross-examinations of each side's witnesses.

The outcome of the contest will, of course, be determined by more than the skills of the cross-examiners. There are other indispensable skills, such as the ability to open and sum up. And the most important ingredient will be the quality of the facts themselves. Nevertheless, the most contentious moments of the trial are likely to occur during cross-examination. So, even while recognizing that there is much to write about in regard to the other important courtroom skills, this is a work devoted to identifying and developing the skills of cross-examination.

Thus, trial advocacy is a critical skill for lawyers to effectively represent their clients, and training is essential since no one is a "born" trial lawyer. It must be studied and then practiced. Lawyers who fail to do this will often feel the need to reach negotiated resolutions rather than face courtroom combat.

To those who agree with me, it seems nonsensical how little time even those who call themselves "litigators" spend developing and exercising important trial muscles such as cross-examination, as compared to other skills like researching and writing. Why is it this way? There are two basic reasons.

First, the United States' legal system does not require lawyers to become specialized as barristers or solicitors as they are in the United Kingdom. Every law school graduate who can pass a bar exam—which itself tests *no* trial skills—becomes licensed to try any and all kinds of cases, from capital crimes to sophisticated class actions. The medical profession is run quite differently. The lives of patients depend upon specialization, so hospitals insist on board certifications. Courts do not. The result is that lawyers are incentivized to present themselves as "skilled trial counsel," skilled or not, with clients left to figure out who really has the courtroom skills.

Second, there has been a well-documented reduction in all types of trials, which has resulted in even less on-the-job training.* But why are there fewer trials? Some argue

---

* Jeffrey Q. Smith and Grant R. MacQueen, "Going, Going, But Not Quite Gone: Trials Continue to Decline in Federal and State Courts. Does it Matter?" *Judicature* 101, no. 4 (Winter 2017), Bolch Judicial Institute, Duke Law School, https://judicature.duke.edu/articles/going -going-but-not-quite-gone-trials-continue-to-decline-in-federal-and -state-courts-does-it-matter/.

that there are fewer criminal trials because mandatory minimums and sentencing guidelines have driven more plea agreements. There is some merit to that, but it does not explain why there are fewer civil trials.

One way to illustrate why there are fewer trials is through the following anecdote. First we had "Trial by Ordeal," where guilt or innocence was determined based on whether God would help the innocent by performing a miracle on their behalf when placing the accused's hand in a fire. We abandoned that after losing too many hands. Then we had "Trial by Combat," where the outcomes of accusations were determined by the winner of a joust between knights. We abandoned that after losing too many knights. And now, we settle disputes through "Pre-Trial Ordeal," in which lawyers get ready to joust, but settle out before the main event, often after client funds have gone the way of hands and knights.

The result of all this is that the lack of training is exacerbated by the lack of practice. And that is a shame, not just for the art of trial advocacy, but for the whole justice system because the trial is the vehicle to bring the truth out. The trial is where an independent trier of fact judges the credibility of everyone before them as different versions of the "truth" are presented and challenged. And what emerges is often unanticipated. Indeed, many lawyers will admit they didn't see the case the same way before trial as they did after it was over. And the unanticipated cross-examinations conducted by the opposing lawyer are often the cause for that failure of foresight.

As Desiderius Erasmus said: "in the land of the blind, the one-eyed man is king." If you learn the skills outlined in this work, you will have a tremendous advantage over the other side, not only in the courtroom, but in the discovery run-up to the trial because the success or failure of a case is often driven from its beginning. Understanding what a case is worth (i.e., seeing what is good and what is problematic) is vital for an advocate advising a client about how to proceed. Understanding the scope of what can be achieved during cross-examination by both sides is indispensable to an evaluation of the entire case. Indeed, the advocate with the longest sightline will be able to make decisions *before* it is too late, unlike the advocate who proceeds with one proverbial foot in front of the other en route to a brick wall.

Not only will the techniques described here make you an effective cross-examiner and, therefore, a more potent advocate, but they will also translate more broadly since these skills permeate almost every walk of life. Indeed, the need to be a persuasive person is not a sometimes thing; it is an all-of-the-time thing. As you shall see, the principles that make for a good courtroom cross-examiner directly correlates to being a persuasive person out of the courtroom. For example, while the rules of conduct may be different in different venues, maintaining credibility drives success or failure in any situation.

PART 1

CHAPTER ONE

You Don't Know How to Cross-Examine (Yet)

There are many important things to learn to become a skilled cross-examiner. However, the one that seems the simplest is actually the hardest to accept: cross-examination is a learned skill like all other aspects of trial advocacy. No one is able to do it well without training.

Having taught the full spectrum, from law students to experienced practitioners, it is repeatedly demonstrated that the failure to accept that this is a learned skill is the greatest impediment toward improvement. The reality is that no one is born an able cross-examiner.

This must be understood for growth to occur. I say the following at the beginning of every class: 1) none of you are good at this yet; and 2) there is no reason that you should be good at something you don't know how to do. Even though everyone nods and agrees with these inarguable truisms, I know that it will not matter once they perform a mock cross-examination.

The problem boils down to failing to appreciate that trial advocacy is a skill just like any other. For example, when I ask students if they can play the guitar without lessons, they readily admit that they cannot since they have not learned how. Anyone can cause a guitar to make noise, but making music requires more. Cross-examination, however, presents an insidious problem: people speak and argue all the time. This leads us to the erroneous belief that we have already used these skills in everyday life. There are two problems with this. First, cross-examining a witness before a trier of fact is not the same thing as arguing at the dinner table. Second, even though we may frequently speak and argue in everyday life, it does not mean that we do it well.

Some say that to become very good at something all we need to do is practice, because practice makes perfect. I disagree. Skiing down a mountain a thousand times without intellectually understanding the best techniques leaves you far from what you could be. Sure, you may pick up a few things in between falls, but your lack of foundational knowledge will impede progress because you will not practice doing things correctly. The same is true with cross-examination. If someone says that they have cross-examined a hundred witnesses, the only thing we know for sure is that they have been down the mountain a hundred times, and not whether they are very good at it.

There is, however, good news: Once we accept that we need help, we are positioned to excel. Accepting this reality, learning the foundations of the skill, and then repeatedly applying the principles are what make a beginner into a skilled practitioner.

CHAPTER TWO
Credibility Is Everything

I promised good news and here it is: Anyone can become very good at cross-examination. I learned at a young age that, no matter how much work was put in, I was not going to be in the NBA or NFL. Many occupations require an innate skill, athletic attribute, or appearance without which we cannot excel or even participate. But trial advocacy and our subject, cross-examination, can be done effectively by anyone.

In order to understand why any lawyer can develop this skill and even excel, let's understand what we are trying to accomplish on cross-examination. Every trier of fact, be it a judge, jury, arbitrator (or a parent listening to their kids), has the same problem: they want to figure out who is telling the truth about the contested events as soon as possible so they can move on with their lives.

This seems simple enough; however, the trier of fact has a problem: There are two sides arguing that the same event or events should result in a different outcome. Thus, the problem lies in determining who among the well-dressed and well-credentialed lawyers is presenting the "truth."

It is this search for the "truth" that compels the trier of fact to heavily scrutinize *everyone's* credibility. Indeed, the advocate is constantly being judged by the trier of fact since they are the face and voice of their respective side. As such, if an advocate calls a witness to testify and that person is not credible, that stain seeps beyond the witness and onto the advocate and their case, as well.

The most important foundational principle to understand about being persuasive before any trier of fact is that the personal credibility of the advocate is of paramount importance. This simply cannot be overstated. And whenever you rise to cross-examine an adverse witness, your credibility, and the credibility of the witness, is at stake. That does not mean that you will challenge the credentials of every witness you cross-examine. Far from it. But we will come to that. Rather, whatever technique you employ (Credibility Attack, Hitchhiking, Limiting), your trier of fact is evaluating the credibility of what you are telling them through the witness.

You may be surprised at the proposition that the perceived personal credibility of the lawyer is a master weapon in the courtroom. But you should not be. Consider this: the trier of fact believes that you actually do know where the truth lies. Indeed, they often believe that you know more than you *actually* do know. They certainly know that you know more than they will be permitted to hear—and that belief is reinforced every time they hear your adversary object to your offer of evidence.

But your trier of fact knows something else about you: you are a paid advocate with a personal stake in the outcome of the case. And that is true even in a *pro bono* case in terms of the reputational gain that victory brings. Therefore, the trier of fact subliminally evaluates whether you are a person of rectitude presenting "truth" or a salesman interested only in "victory." Therefore, should your personal credibility be damaged in an exchange with a witness, it will take an enormous effort to re-establish it—if that is even possible. Trial lawyers should protect their credibility and never be reckless with it.

Even when making objections, the objector's credibility is on the line. Some lawyers consistently object, even to non-material issues, apparently believing that they are accomplishing two things: 1) that they look strong; and 2) that they are harming the opposing party's ability to prove their case. Not only is neither true—it is far worse. Immaterial objections cause self-inflicted damage over things that don't even matter.

Remember, the trier of fact wants to figure out who is right. The objector now puts themselves in the position of trying to keep information out. This is, of course, something that needs to be done when the issue matters and if there is a basis to believe the objection will be successful. To risk losing an objection over something that may reasonably affect the outcome of the case is a risk that must be taken. To risk losing an objection over things that don't matter reveals an advocate who does not understand the importance of their credibility.

The list of these kinds of credibility sins is endless. Everything an advocate does—from what to say, what not to say, which witnesses to call, and how to deal with those who testify—will affect the credibility of the advocate. Indeed, the truly wise advocate looks to make concessions, when it does not affect the outcome, to earn additional credibility for the struggles ahead that are more important to the outcome.

CHAPTER THREE

(Don't) Give 'Em the Old Razzle Dazzle

*Razzle dazzle 'em
And they'll never catch wise!*[1]

"Razzle Dazzle" from the musical *Chicago* perfectly explains how *not* to think about advocating one's case to the trier of fact. Put simply, substance is how we win, not style or by employing theatrics and deception. Remember: Don't be witty; don't be clever; don't be smart; just be right. And don't follow the previous advice of *Chicago*'s Billy Flynn, Esq.

I firmly believe that triers of fact want to get the case right in the end. It is why people willingly engage in our system of resolving disputes. Now, nothing is absolute, and I can't say that it is impossible to have a trier of fact with an agenda. That being said, an aberrational apple does not ruin the whole barrel.

Going beyond style, we must earn the confidence of the people we are trying to persuade by dealing with *all* of the facts of the case. Yet, what are the *facts*? The facts are what you conclude that the jury will certainly believe.

We must accept the reality that if we minimize or ignore the facts of the case and perform a side-show, we will most likely lose, and deservedly so.

CHAPTER FOUR

How Are We Going to Learn to Cross-Examine?

While it is vital to understand that being the most credible advocate is the foundation for success, we must build on that foundation. We have to learn the techniques available to the cross-examiner as they evaluate whether those tools will enable them to successfully deliver the message to the trier of fact. Think of it like sailing. If your boat isn't aimed in the right direction, it doesn't matter how good you are at working the wind: you will still end up on the rocks. On the other hand, if your boat is aimed in the right direction, but you don't know how to work the wind . . . you will also end up on the rocks. It is only when both strategy and techniques come together that you successfully get where you want to go.

The following chapters lay out the various tools of cross-examination at your disposal to persuasively argue your case through the witness. I have endeavored to separate the various techniques into their own standalone concepts to make them easier to digest. But they are all part of one tool belt, inextricably intertwined with each other.

After we have explored the various techniques at our disposal, we will then move into the three case studies.

These case studies are the critical next step to learn how to cross-examine since they put all of our theoretical principles into the context of reality and define the limits of what we can hope to achieve. After reviewing the case studies, I advise reviewing the strategy and techniques again since they will take on enhanced clarity after having seen them in application. Cross-examination is like most other things in life: the more we work at it, the more we can see and thereby learn.

CHAPTER FIVE

Be a Trained Version of Yourself

The best advocates do not rely upon any kind of artificial delivery mechanism for success. This is not to say that they all act the same way. They don't. But they don't for a good reason—they are all different people. The key point is to be natural, without artifice or trying to imitate anyone else. When doing a cross-examination, I do not change my personality. I talk like me, gesture like me, and stand like me. I don't imitate anyone else, and no one should try and imitate me.

If you try to imitate someone else or put on an artifice based on what you think people want, you will likely destroy your credibility. This includes "acting like a lawyer." People can smell an act a mile away, and the trier of fact is on high alert. Think back to your own real life experiences where you felt that someone was behaving artificially and how you reacted. Did you find them compelling or did you discount the substance of what they had to say, even before hearing it?

I have seen far too many students critiqued on the method of delivery. Put your hand in your pocket, take your hand out of your pocket, use bigger words, use smaller words, gesture more . . . so on and so forth. These things are not the issue and will not decide the outcome of a case. The outcome will be decided based on who is more credible and who understands what really matters to the case and what does not.

CHAPTER SIX
Length Is Irrelevant

One of the hardest things for anyone, especially lawyers, to do is not speak. Whether professionally or socially, some people view silence as a sign of weakness in the face of an adversary arguing against your position. On the other hand, people also tend to needlessly worry about speaking too long and losing the listener's attention.

Because of these two issues, I am commonly asked how long someone's cross-examination should be. It is, of course, impossible to answer this within the paradigm of the question. Instead, the answer is always the same: the length should be no more and no less than you need to make the points that matter. That could mean anything from asking no questions at all to pursuing a multi-day cross-examination. The relevant evidence is what determines how long a cross-examination should be between that wide chasm.

If you have been hurt by a witness and have nothing productive to use, then you should ask nothing because the alternative is worse. While there is a strong temptation to conduct a cross-examination to make the trier of fact think that it wasn't so bad, turning it into a sideshow will quickly take the situation from bad to worse because you will imperil your credibility for a lost cause.

If you have a lot of important evidence to utilize with the witness, then that drives the length of the cross-examination. On the other hand, you may have a small amount of material to use with a witness, but the witness may say unexpected things which will change the length of the cross-examination. We will return to this thought.

The salient point is that we cannot think of a cross-examination or any other aspect of trial advocacy in terms of length. The length does not matter. The only thing that does matter is what you have to say. If you say important things, the trier of fact will be interested and you will be rewarded. You can keep people interested as long as you are interesting. Bathroom breaks may be in order, but your refreshed audience will not bridle at returning.*

---

* If you harbor any doubt that people prefer listening to something lengthy but interesting, as compared to something short but uninteresting, a simple test can be performed by watching *The Godfather* and *The Godfather: Part II* back to back vs. watching *National Lampoon's: Gold Diggers.*

CHAPTER SEVEN

Identify the Important Evidence

As we have discussed, the best advocates don't rely upon any performance artifice, and they certainly don't try to hoodwink the trier of fact. Instead, they do exactly the opposite. They act naturally and don't make things up. Rather than try to run a sideshow, they rely upon the power of the evidence and wield the Rule of Probability to control the witness and, in turn, persuade the trier of fact. We will cover the Rule of Probability in Chapter 17.

There is an old expression: "You can have all the good lawyers; I'll take the good facts." None of us can turn water into wine, and none of us can make a structurally terrible argument great. If you catch your child red-handed taking a cookie out of the cookie jar, the best lawyer in the world won't convince you it didn't happen.

It is instead those situations where the outcome is not clear that the quality of the advocate really matters. Advocates cannot control the structure of the dispute, but we can make the most of what we have. To do that, we must be able to determine what evidence is helpful, what is harmful, and what is irrelevant. Understanding what matters doesn't sound like it should be difficult, but it is. It may be the most difficult of all the tasks confronting the trial lawyer. I am surely not alone in witnessing advocates fail to see something good or bad about their case that later appears to have been staring them in the face.

All litigants naturally suffer from tunnel vision about their cases because it is unnatural to see a case from all sides when we are emotionally invested in one particular side. This emotional tunnel vision must nevertheless be overcome so that the advocate can understand what evidence has value, good or bad, and then discern how to deal with it. The way to see the case dispassionately is by first understanding why this happens and then learning how to stress test the evidence from all sides with an emotional thumb off the scales.

Do Not Follow Sammy's Rule

No, I have not named a rule after myself, but it was instead named after me. The story goes that when I was a little boy, I apparently believed that no one could see me if shut my eyes. Precocious, indeed.

This principle, however, also applies to other humans, albeit in a much more insidious manner than a child physically covering their own eyes. Instead, Sammy's Rule manifests itself subconsciously in the minds of most adults. And this tendency is heightened when we become litigants and even their advocates. The problem is that we become so invested in our side of an argument that we don't want to see the other side's point of view. So we don't.

Abraham Lincoln well understood how we become intellectually blinded by our emotions when he famously said, "A man who represents himself has a fool for a client." But this is an issue which also affects advocates, as well. If you doubt this is true, look no further than our everyday lives where people routinely make arguments which simply ignore the evidence that is hurtful, allowing the other side to point it out and gain ground. This does not happen because people want to make bad arguments, but because they are emotionally unable to see problems which undermine positions they are invested in. Simply put, it is an issue of emotion rather than intellect.

There is perhaps no more poignant example than our current political scene and the desire to seek news information from sources which will buttress our existing opinions. And why is that? Because neither deeply dug-in side wants to hear that the other side's point of view has merit. Democrats don't want MSNBC to bolster Republican ideas any more than Republicans want Fox News to talk about how great the Democrats are doing. And so they don't.

While this issue affects everyone to some degree, advocates must nevertheless learn to overcome it in order to effectively cross-examine. We have to learn how to look at the material from all sides without bias so that we can see the information for what it is, not what we want it to be. We must imagine ourselves as the other side and objectively see things through their lens to understand their argument and what evidence will support it. Then we can make a truly professional judgment of how the trier of fact will evaluate all of the information in the case and what we can reasonably hope to achieve in selling our case through the cross-examinations of the witnesses called against us.

After seeing the world from the other side, we can stress test the potential evidence to see what is good for us, what is bad for us, and what is irrelevant. One of the best methods is to work through it with someone else. Analyzing the material in your own head is certainly possible as you learn how to look at the evidence from all sides. However, the best way to learn how to see things from both sides is by having someone else propound the opposing argument. Applying pressure either makes diamonds or rubble.

CHAPTER EIGHT

Don't Read the Questions

It is, of course, perfectly natural to want to script things out, but that is not possible with cross-examination. It is not possible because you will often be dealing with witnesses who are uninterested in making your life easy and are likely to say unexpected things. Not only is reading written questions impossible, but it is also ill-advised because reading from a script damages your credibility and thus your persuasiveness.*

Think about all of the times you have seen someone reading from a script and how you felt: bored and unpersuaded by their lack of eye contact and carefully curated remarks. This is why politicians use teleprompters: to make it seem as if they are not reading from a script. They appear to be maintaining eye contact and are able to give the illusion that they are speaking extemporaneously, even though they are not. This makes them appear more genuine and persuasive than if they were reading with their heads down or constantly toggling their heads up and down.

---

* This is true, as well, for opening statements and summations where it is at least possible to read from scripts (which should not be done), but it is not even possible to do such a reading in the give and take of a cross-examination.

Reflect instead on those people who you know are not reading from a script and how much more engaging and persuasive they are. You will be more persuasive in every walk of life if you do not read when delivering information to others, and cross-examination is certainly no exception. Indeed, it is even more critical in cross-examination than in a speech or a movie because cross-examination is a live adversarial exercise between two people, and there are no second takes. Moreover, it is essential in a trial to keep your head up to observe the reactions of the witness as well as any effect on the trier of fact.

You may be thinking: well, if it is so clear, then why do so many people write down and read to their own detriment? They do it out of fear that they will not have the words to say when the time comes and so choose the lesser of the two perceived evils. Now, there is nothing wrong with writing things out in advance if that helps to clarify the information in your own mind. The issue turns on whether writing things down is a preparation tool or if it becomes a crutch that you become unable to speak without.

I do not script things out in advance and will only make bullet points of what I want to communicate to the trier of fact through the witness. I have never read them out during a cross-examination, and they are created only for the purpose of organizing the harvestable information from the witness or the points to be made *through* the witness to the trier of fact.

Everyone is able to communicate information to friends, family, and even total strangers without reading from notes. This is proven every day of our lives. If you want to find out what your children had for lunch, you know how to ask the relevant questions without reading from scripted notes. Once we know *what* we want to say, we will have no problem saying it in any forum. The words will come. They always do everywhere else, and they will in a judicial forum, as well.

CHAPTER NINE

Preparing the "Questions"

Your cross-examination "questions" should most often be statements made by you through the witness to the trier of fact which the court reporter decorates with question marks. Therefore, your pre-trial cross-examination outline will often not be questions, but instead the points you want to make. The structure of the eventual statement will come to you when you recall the point to be made or see the note in your outline.

A different problem arises if you take notes while the witness is testifying on direct examination. As we shall see, problems arise because of the way many cross-examiners take notes during the witness's direct-examination. Unfortunately, many trial lawyers preparing to cross-examine take a pen and draw a line down the middle of the page. On one side—usually the left—they keep a running count of what the witness says. On the other side, they make a note of what they are going to cross-examine on. Both sides of the page are a disaster.

If you write a running account of virtually everything the witness says, you are forced to keep your head down rather than up—thus missing observing the telltale signs from all the *dramatis personae* in the courtroom. The left side of the page will be largely useless since you are *not* intending to cross-examine on things from that side of the page. That's all the stuff on the right hand side of the page.

But the right side of the page has its own problems. Your notes for cross-examination are now nailed into the order and organization of the direct examination—which is not likely to be your preferred order for cross-examination since your opponent's order and organization was likely constructed to enhance the persuasiveness of *their* argument. As we shall see later, a cardinal principle of advocacy is that the order and organization of what you have to say is as persuasive as the content itself. We will return to this principle in Chapter 12.

But for purposes of note taking, the open question is: If we shouldn't draw the line down the middle of the page, if we shouldn't write down a running account of the direct examination, and if we shouldn't write down our questions, what *should* our notes look like as we listen to the direct examination? Only write what you intend to cross-examine on.

What should you write? The answer of the witness as close to word-for-word as you can manage. And only one note on a page. Why? Because you want to integrate those notes into your prepared line of cross-examination. One note—one page—and off. Then integrate. And when you come to ask the question about it, that question will likely begin, "you said on direct . . . ", "I wrote down your words . . . ", "but isn't it a fact that . . ."

CHAPTER TEN

Hear the Witness

Hear the witness? You may be saying to yourself, *is the next chapter about keeping your eyes open?* I acknowledge that advising someone to hear the witness's answers to the questions seems obvious. It is, however, unfortunately anything but. Instead, this is one of the most significant problems that cross-examiners face. Indeed, we will see many examples in our case studies where cross-examiners simply ignore important information in the witness's answers. Why don't cross-examiners hear the answer? Usually because they are worried about forming their next question.

This issue reminds me of the scene from the film *White Men Can't Jump* where Wesley Snipes's character exclaims to Woody Harrelson's character: "Look, man, you can listen to Jimi [Hendrix] but you can't hear him. There's a difference. Just because you're listening to him doesn't mean you're hearing him."[2]

This frequently happens on cross-examination. Our ears listen to the sounds of the witness's answer to know when to begin the next question, but we do not process the implication of the answer to the case and adjust accordingly in real time. Thus, instead of responding to what the witness said, the cross-examiner ignores it and continues on the pre-planned journey, notwithstanding the fact that the situation has changed, sometimes for the worse, but often times for the better.

Why does this happen and how can we deal with it? First, no matter how well-planned out, a cross-examination is an adversarial and dynamic event between two people, both of whose credibility will be studied by the trier of fact.

Second, the cross-examiner has the tougher job setting the table to control the witness through the content of the question after that witness has already testified on direct examination. Thus, the cross-examiner already has a lot to process apart from any deviations that the witness may suddenly take along the way. As such, these sudden deviations can become overwhelming for many cross-examiners to handle and thus they are ignored. And this problem is exacerbated by the way many cross-examiners prepare for the cross-examination and then take notes during the direct examination, as we previously discussed.

As you see, your cross-examination questions are very often statements by you designed to force the witness into agreement with the premise of the question, at the pain of being disbelieved by the trier of fact. Now, sometimes witnesses will choose to be evasive rather than agree with things they don't want to. As we shall see in our case studies, witnesses will often choose the path of evasion even though it hurts their own credibility. When this happens, it is not a burden for the cross-examiner, but instead a tremendous gift. But this is only true if the cross-examiner hears the answer and makes the witness pay for it. How do you make the witness pay? There are different techniques depending on the nature of the evasion, which we will fully discuss in Chapter 15.

CHAPTER ELEVEN

The Content of the Question Controls the Witness

So, credibility is everything, we should not read our questions from a script, and we should hear the witness's answers: but how do we control an adverse witness called by the other side who probably does not want to help us? The answer is: we control a witness through the content of the question, not its form.

The traditional view has been that we must use leading questions on cross-examination to control a witness and to keep them from saying things we don't want to hear. The theory goes even further: We should demand that the witness only answer yes or no on cross-examination. This theory is, however, problematic for two reasons.

First, it is impossible to always keep a witness confined to simple yes or no answers. Witnesses will often seek to add context to their answers to defend themselves from the questioning. If the cross-examiner seeks the judge's help to force the witness to answer with a simple yes or no, they are unlikely to get consistent help because many questions cannot be answered with a simple yes or no. Even when they can, judges often permit witnesses to elaborate. And when a cross-examiner seeks help from the judge and doesn't receive it, the jury sees the judge side with the witness, and the cross-examiner is left with a witness who has learned that the cross-examiner is not in control.

Second, even if we could confine a witness to simple "yes" or "no" answers, we wouldn't want to because the perceived over-control of a witness damages the cross-examiner's credibility. Remember, the trier of fact wants to figure out who is telling the truth. A cross-examiner who refuses to allow a witness to answer a question beyond a single word will rightly be viewed as frightened that the witness has harmful information and that the attorney is trying to keep the "truth" from the trier of fact. Even temporary success in stifling the witness can be harmful, because the other side will be allowed to re-direct. And when the other side says, "Now, Mrs. X, remember when opposing counsel stopped you from explaining what happened, please make a full answer," the same information will be elicited on re-direct that the cross-examiner sought to suppress. The credibility damage from the failed suppression may do more harm than the actual information, which still needs to be dealt with in any event.

As we will discuss, there are times to use leading questions and there are times not to. However, choosing the form of the question is just a method of delivery, not a tool of control. Control over the witness comes instead from the cross-examiner's selection of the content of the questions in conjunction with the availability of impeachment material such as prior inconsistent statements or pieces of evidence. And even when there is no physical evidence

with which to confront the witness, there is the omnipres-
ent Rule of Probability to wield in appropriate situations.
This we will come to shortly.

CHAPTER TWELVE
Organization Enhances Persuasiveness

We have already touched on how to achieve the organization you desire for your cross-examination. But that merely deals with implementing the selected strategy. Now we must go deeper and try to identify why it is that the order of what we hear impacts its effectiveness.

There are many schools of thought about how to organize cross-examination arguments. Some subscribe to the primacy/recency method of putting the best material first and last so that the good stuff sticks in the mind of the trier of fact. Some organize a cross-examination by following the witness's direct examination sequence. I disagree with both of these processes. The order of what we say is as important as what we have to say because each piece of evidence can potentially enhance other pieces, which together enhances the entire argument.

Let's first deal with re-walking in the direct examination's footsteps. Why is this a frequent choice of cross-examiners? As noted, one reason is because of the way the cross-examiner made notes during the direct examination. Thus, the order becomes the route of inquiry. This, however, forces the cross-examiner into the order of the direct examiner. Another reason this occurs is that most cross-examiners don't really understand how to organize the different areas of the cross-examination and thus following the direct examination is the path of least resistance. Whatever its cause, we must reject this method.

We should never blithely follow the order of the direct examination because we are sublimating a critical tool of our power of persuasion to the other side. It bears repeating: the order and organization of what you have to say is as persuasive as what you have to say. Therefore, not only would failing to select our own persuasive order abandon an important tool, but it would also select our adversary's organizational choices, which were made to make *their* case more persuasive, not ours.

While this follow-the-leader tactic has no rational curb appeal, the primacy/recency theory does at first blush, since we are at least still maintaining some decision making about the organization. Indeed, we all have likely found merit in the theory that "you never get a second chance to make a first impression." While this theory is certainly better than playing follow-the-leader, it is also nevertheless flawed because it dictates order and organization based upon a psychological evaluation of the trier of fact rather than based on the material itself.

Now don't get me wrong: I am a strong proponent of starting off strong and finishing strong. But I am also a big fan of being strong all of the time. While some of our cross-examination material may be better than other parts, that is not what drives organization. Instead, the organization is determined by what material best supports other material in order to make the entire argument more persuasive.

An excellent illustration of this point occurs when the prosecution in a criminal case calls an associate of the defendant to the stand—and that witness has his own criminal record. The prosecutor knows that they would be wise to bring that record out themselves—and not leave it for the defense attorney to spring out on cross-examination, implying that the prosecutor has concealed it. But the question is: Should the prosecutor bring out the bad stuff at the outset, the middle, or at the very end of their direct?

The foolish prosecutor does not bring the bad stuff out at any point, imperiling their credibility. The silly prosecutor brings it out in the middle, hoping that the end of the direct examination will overcome it with the middle information put aside. The wise prosecutor puts that kind of stuff at the end of the direct examination. They do not want the trier of fact hearing the testimony of the witness through the lens of the witness's harmful credibility information. The prosecutor wants the jurors rowing in the boat, believing the testimony before they have to confront those jurors with the unwholesome background of the witness. If the jurors already believe the witness, they will be more likely to forgive deficiencies.

But what about the defense attorney? They would usually *begin* their examination with the nasty stuff about the witness. They want to diminish the credibility of the witness before they have to confront the credibility of what the witness has said about their client. Indeed, they may even have objected to the prosecutor bringing out the bad stuff—on the ground that the prosecution is impeaching their own witness—not because they want to suppress the information, but because they want to make it appear that the prosecutor has.

The goal is to use the power of order and organization to make the entire argument stronger. We must reject the rigid principle of "always do this" or "always do that" since we operate in a dynamic environment where the only constant is our desire to be more persuasive and always protect our credibility.

CHAPTER THIRTEEN
The Forms of Cross-Examination Questions

As previously noted, control of the witness is exercised by the content of the question, not its form. The selection of a leading or a non-leading question turns on which will be more persuasive to the trier of fact, given its content. The selection should not be driven by fear of the witness.

Let's use a simple fact pattern to demonstrate how to use leading and non-leading questions. We will also build upon this hypothetical to explore other techniques. Remember that this fact pattern is only a vehicle to see the tangible application of the techniques. Regard it as the martial arts Wing Chun wooden training dummy that Bruce Lee practiced on. We are not trying the case, but rather exploring and practicing technique.

The situation is as follows: Mr. A is accused of punching Mr. B in the face. Mr. A claims that it was another person that punched Mr. B. There is a witness who claims he saw Mr. A punch Mr. B, but there is indisputable evidence that the witness was standing fifty yards away and was behind the person who punched Mr. B.

The objective for Mr. A's attorney is to demonstrate that the witness's identification of Mr. A as the attacker is not credible. The tool we have to undermine the identification of Mr. A is the indisputable evidence showing the witness's distance and vantage point.

Leading Questions

A leading question is designed to suggest the answer in the form of the question. The simplest way to think of it is to state the answer you want to hear and then put a question mark at the end. For example, if you want someone to admit it is raining outside, you would ask, "It is raining outside" and then add an "isn't it" or "correct" at the end of the sentence. Now to our sample fact pattern with a limit of four cross-examination questions:

Q: You're 100 percent positive you saw Mr. A punch Mr. B?

A: Yes.

Q: You're 100 percent positive even though you were fifty yards away when it happened?

A: Yes.

Q: You're 100 percent positive it was Mr. A even though your view was only of the back side of the person who punched Mr. B?

A: Yes. Mr. A's rear profile looks like the person I saw punch Mr. B.

Q: You're 100 percent positive Mr. A punched Mr. B even though you never saw his face and were standing half a football field away at the time?

A: Yes.

This is not a bad cross-examination in four questions. The witness is not going to fall over and admit that the identification is wrong. Instead, the goal is to persuade the trier of fact that the witness's identification is unreliable, notwithstanding the witness's insistence. Now, let's compare the same line of questioning, but with a different form of the questions.

Controlled Open-Ended Questions

To be clear, we are not interested in pure open-ended questions, but that is true on direct examination as well. The trial is not a time to conduct discovery or to delve inside the mind of the witness and see what comes out. Questions that we don't know the answer to and which we aren't sure can't hurt us are of no interest.

The problem is that no one, to my knowledge, has defined a third type of question that exists between the open-ended question and the leading question. Therefore, we will call it the controlled open-ended question.

A controlled open-ended question is a question that sounds like an open-ended question, but is not because you know the answer and have the ability to control the witness if they deviate from the evidence. The controlled open-ended question can also apply even if you don't know the answer to the question, but are sure that there is no answer that can hurt you.

Now let's compare our leading questions example to the one using controlled open-ended questions:

Q: How sure are you that Mr. A punched Mr. B?
A: I am 100 percent sure.

Q: How far away were you when you made this identification that you're 100 percent sure about?

A: I was fifty yards away when it happened.

Q: From your view fifty yards away, what did the
assailant's face look like when he punched Mr. B?

A: Well, I didn't actually see his face. I never saw the
front side of his body, but Mr. A's rear profile looks
like the person I saw punch Mr. B.

Q: You're 100 percent positive Mr. A punched Mr. B
even though you never saw his face and were standing half a football field away at the time?

A: Yes.

I am confident that this is the more persuasive cross-examination even though it has elicited the same information
as the leading one. But why? It is more persuasive because
the form of the questions forces the witness to say the bad
things in their own voice instead of with a simple yes or no.*

The best part is, not only is this more persuasive, but
there is also no downside if you construct the questions
consistently with the evidence. If you don't have either the
evidence or the Rule of Probability to persuade the trier of
fact, then you will be unsuccessful regardless of the question's form. To wit, if the witness was standing five feet
away and had a frontal view of the puncher, then there is
no form of question that will help you.

---

* Note that I have constructed the witness's answer in the light most
favorable to them under the circumstances while still protecting their
credibility. This of course does not account for the very real possibility
that the witness would make unforced errors and damage their credibility by being evasive.

Let's do a deeper dissection into how I chose the content of these questions. This witness is not going to admit that he was wrong, so the name of the game is to convince the trier of fact that, while this witness thinks he is right, his view was not good enough to make a reliable identification.

Question #1: How sure are you that Mr. A punched Mr. B?

I didn't know the answer to the question, but no answer could hurt me. Maybe the witness will decide to pick something other than 100 percent since he is worried about the distance and the view-point questions he knows are coming. If so, that is good for me since it will indicate a less reliable identification. If the witness chooses 100 percent (as is most likely) and insists on total surety, then I am no worse off and can use it against the witness by juxtaposing it against the viewpoint issues. Either way, no answer can hurt me, and there is a chance that good things can happen if the witness decides to play games.

Question #2: How far away were you when made this identification that you're 100 percent sure about?

I know the answer to this question and am forcing the witness to acknowledge one of the two pieces of evidence I have to undermine his credibility. I also intentionally incorporate the 100 percent figure to try and judo his complete certainty against the facts to undermine his credibility.

Question #3: From your view fifty yards away, what did the assailant's face look like when he punched Mr. B?

I know the answer to this question and deliberately structured it to emphasize the point. Knowing that the witness never saw the puncher's face, the question assumes that someone making a 100 percent positive identification must have seen the person's face. I know the answer, and the witness knows the answer. The only choice he has is to admit something that he knows undermines his credibility, or to make things even worse (but better for me) by trying to play games.

Question #4: You're 100 percent positive Mr. A punched Mr. B even though you never saw his face and were standing half a football field away at the time?

This is the same question that I used for the leading question example. I chose it here because it works well in tying everything together after the series of controlled open-ended questions. Notice how Question #4 is more persuasive in the second cross-examination even though it is the same question. This is because the first three questions of the second cross-examination did not over-control the witness with leading questions. The leading question at the end then ties everything together and packs a punch.

We should reject the notion that one kind of question should be used all of the time and that other types should never be used. These types of questions are simply tools in your arsenal for arguing your case through the witness and persuading the trier of fact.

CHAPTER FOURTEEN
Looping

Looping is the technique where we re-incorporate information from a previous answer into the next question. The value of looping is two-fold. First, it reminds the trier of fact of helpful information that was previously elicited. Second, it builds up your argument over a series of questions to make it more persuasive. But why is that more persuasive?

Because things become more or less persuasive due to the other attendant facts and circumstances. Thus, when multiple facts are stitched together, it creates a mosaic of probabilities that is more powerful than if the single pieces were offered on their own. Notice how this concept ties in with our organization principle of using different pieces of information to support the other parts to create a stronger overall argument.

Let's look back at our demonstrative cross-examination utilizing the controlled open-ended questions:

Q: How sure are you that Mr. A punched Mr. B?
A: I am 100 percent sure.
Q: How far away were you when made this identification that you're 100 percent sure about?
A: I was fifty yards away when it happened.

Here I have chosen to loop the "100 percent sure" answer back into the question. Now, I could ask how far away he was without it. But because I know that most reasonable people would consider this a long distance away, looping it back in makes his answer less credible since that level of distance and that level of certainty are potentially problematic together.

> Q: From your view fifty yards away, what did the assailant's face look like when he punched Mr. B?
> A: Well, I didn't actually see his face. I never saw the front side of his body, but Mr. A's rear profile looks like the person I saw punch Mr. B.

I have now looped the "fifty yards away" answer back into the question because it compounds his next problem: he never saw the assailant's face.

> Q: You're 100 percent positive Mr. A punched Mr. B even though you never saw his face and were standing half a football field away at the time?
> A: Yes.

Here I have chosen to loop all of the previous problematic answers back into the question in one bitter pill for him to swallow. And for good measure, I have amplified his "fifty yards" answer into "half a football field away" to enhance the context, which turns the screw even more.

CHAPTER FIFTEEN
The Three Types of Cross-Examination

As discussed, the purpose of cross-examination is to persuasively argue your case through the witness, and we have discussed the tools available to accomplish this. But between the high-level strategic purpose of protecting our credibility and lower-level techniques for formulating the questions, there is also a mid-layer technique to understand.

A common error of cross-examiners is assuming that every witness is a nail to be hammered. Indeed, hard-hitting and punishing cross-examinations are what commonly come to mind when people think of cross-examination—the proverbial mano a mano high noon showdown where the witness is revealed to be a liar. Sometimes this actually happens, of course, but far less than people assume. It is critical to accurately diagnose how to deal with each witness because you will damage your own credibility if you attack a witness as a liar and the trier of fact concludes otherwise.

There are three separate techniques for dealing with a witness on cross-examination. They are not mutually exclusive. Depending on the testimony of the witness, the evidence in the case, and the Rule of Probability, you may utilize one, two, or even all three of them during the same cross-examination. It is all situation-dependent.

Credibility Attack

This is what you came for, the main event. I like to analogize it to being in the Thunderdome (from the film *Mad Max Beyond Thunderdome*) as a reminder of just how dangerous it is to our own credibility. In the film, the Thunderdome is a steel cage contest where the only rule is that "Two men enter, one man leaves."[3]

A Credibility Attack cross-examination is similar because when the cross-examiner challenges the credibility of the witness, they are simultaneously wagering their own credibility. The cross-examiner's assertion and the witness's denial force the trier of fact to choose. And the trier of fact does so with each assertion and denial as they happen, not waiting for the case to end. Indeed, the details of this confrontation will be only imperfectly recalled by the end of the case, if at all. But the impression as to whether the lawyer or the witness was the truth giver will likely last.

While these contests are very exciting, they are also very dangerous, since the cross-examiner's credibility may not survive the encounter. The more important the issue being contested, the larger the fall for the losing side.*

---

* This type of cross-examination is generally referred to as impeachment, but impeachment is actually a specific tactic for going after the credibility of a witness (i.e., to use a prior statement against the witness). The choice of nomenclature aside, the issues are the same, and this is where cross-examiners get themselves most in trouble.

This doesn't mean you should be afraid of attacking the honesty of a witness's testimony, but only to ensure you understand how important this type of cross-examination is to your own credibility and the outcome of the case.

So, how do we effectively do a Credibility Attack cross-examination? As detailed in our previous mock cross-examination, we have to accurately diagnose the situation and then use the evidence and our available tactics to cast doubt upon the witness's assertions. This does not always mean that you need to prove that the witness is intentionally lying, although that may be the case. Often times, a witness takes a position that needs to be refuted, but you do not need to take on the additional burden of proving that they are intentionally lying, rather than mistaken or simply unsure.

Let's look back to our hypothetical cross-examination using controlled open-ended questions:

Q: How sure are you that Mr. A punched Mr. B?

A: I am 100 percent sure.

Q: How far away were you when you made this identification that you're 100 percent sure about?

A: I was fifty yards away when it happened.

Q: From your view fifty yards away, what did the assailant's face look like when he punched Mr. B?

A: Well, I didn't actually see his face. I never saw the front side of his body, but Mr. A's rear profile looks like the person I saw punch Mr. B.

Q: You're 100 percent positive Mr. A punched Mr. B even though you never saw his face and were standing half a football field away at the time?

A: Yes.

We shouldn't take on the higher burden of proving that this witness was intentionally lying when we don't have to. The correct diagnosis is that, while the witness's testimony must be refuted or the defendant will be convicted, it is only possible (and also easier) to attack his version of events by demonstrating that he is unintentionally wrong due to the circumstances. If we go too far (i.e., without evidentiary support), and claim that he is intentionally lying, we will lose the credibility fight.

After correctly diagnosing that this witness must be refuted, but does not need to be proven to be an intentional liar, we have to decide how we are going to demonstrate that his version of events is not believable. In this case, we used the form of the questions and the evidence about distance and viewpoint to argue through the witness that his identification is unreliable.

There are other tactics available to argue through the witness that their version of events is not credible. We can confront them with their prior sworn statements or with any possible contradictory evidence to disprove their version of events. Every situation will be different in its particulars, but the principles for dealing with it will be the same.

Hitchhiking

It is often the case that a witness has more information than what he or she testified to on direct examination. Often, at least some of that information can be helpful to your case. Certainly a defendant on the stand is your sworn enemy if you are the plaintiff or the prosecutor, since parties usually arrange their testimony so that they will win the case if believed. This type of witness forces Credibility Attack cross-examinations. But many witnesses do have helpful things to say for both sides of a dispute. The Hitchhiking technique is what we use to bring out those helpful things.

Indeed, because many witnesses have both helpful and harmful information, one of the challenging things in putting on a case is deciding which witnesses to call after considering their pluses and minuses. Deciding how to balance the bitter and the sweet is part of the process.

As an illustration, let's look back at our hypothetical cross-examination, but let's add another fact to the situation using the same witness who claims to have seen Mr. A punch Mr. B. Now that same witness also has information that he previously saw Mr. B in the area acting belligerently in what appeared to be an inebriated state.

Let's assume that our defense theory remains that the identification was inaccurate and that Mr. A did not punch Mr. B (as opposed to a self-defense theory). This witness and his information will prove helpful in making the argument that someone else punched the victim since his conduct likely offended many different people.

As such, we should employ the Hitchhiking strategy while remaining careful not to affect our own credibility. This is another reason why it is important to correctly diagnose this witness as mistaken rather than a liar. It allows us to more effectively use the helpful information while discrediting the bad information at the same time. Here is an example of the Hitchhiking section of the cross-examination using three controlled open-ended questions:

> **Q:** Did you see Mr. B before he was punched in the face?
> **A:** Yes, I saw him in the same area around thirty minutes earlier.
> **Q:** What was he doing when you saw him?
> **A:** He was sitting on a bench and yelling at people as they passed by.
> **Q:** Was his speech slurred when he was yelling at people?
> **A:** Yes, it was.

As we previously saw, this witness has harmful information which must be neutralized. But he also has helpful information which we can use to argue our theory that someone else punched Mr. B. It may be that a witness only has bad information, or it may be that they only have good information, or a bit of both. Every case and every witness is different. But once we correctly diagnose the witness and understand the available evidence, we can utilize these tactics and strategies to argue our case through a witness called by the other side.

Limiting

It is sometimes said that "what you don't know can't hurt you." That can be true. But it can also be true that "what you don't know *can* hurt you." Using this concept, the Limiting strategy can be used to show that the witness does not know important things about the case.

Demonstrating gaps in knowledge can result in a variety of outcomes, ranging from showing the irrelevance of the witness's testimony to arguing your theory of the case through the witness.

Let's again use our hypothetical fact pattern and ask three cross-examination questions:

> Q: Did you see the events leading up to Mr. B being punched in the face?
> A: No, I didn't.
> Q: Did you hear what was said between Mr. B and the person who punched him in the face before the punch was thrown?
> A: No, I didn't.
> Q: So, you don't know anything about the events leading up to Mr. B being punched in the face other than that Mr. B was acting belligerently and appeared inebriated?
> A: That's right.

The last answer was compelled by the Rule of Probability, and we used all three techniques in one cross-examination. We used the Credibility Attack technique to undermine the reliability of his identification, we used the Hitchhiking technique to bring out the good information, and we used the Limiting technique to show what the witness doesn't know and to argue an alternative theory: that someone else punched Mr. A given his belligerent conduct and intoxicated state. While each of these techniques was strong on its own, they become even stronger when put together into an organized argument.

CHAPTER SIXTEEN
Pulling the Chain

Some may be thinking: "it looks pretty easy when everything goes according to plan, but what about when the witness isn't cooperative." It's, of course, a fair point since things probably won't go according to plan because witnesses will say things that you do not expect.

However, you should not be afraid of witnesses who deviate from saying things that the evidence and the Rules of Probability compel them to admit. To the contrary, when a witness plays games, you are given the opportunity to bring them back in line and damage their credibility, while also making your point. Think of these moments as a two- or three-for-one special at the credibility bank.

So why do witnesses consistently make the mistake of evasion instead of conceding where they must? This is the result of emotion overtaking logic. Even non-party witnesses called by one side may become entrenched in their positions. And when they do become entrenched, they see where a line of questioning is going and attempt to play games to avoid difficult moments.

As our case studies will reveal, there are many different ways that witnesses can evade giving answers. These range from outright falsehoods to unclear half answers to answers which don't answer the question at all. When the witness employs these evasion tactics, we must remind them, in the words of the great Joe Lewis: "they can run, but they can't hide."

It is shocking how often cross-examiners let witnesses play these games and don't take advantage of the opportunity to make them pay for it. As we discussed earlier, the failure to actively hear the witness's answer and to have the dexterity to deal with it is a primary culprit. Another reason is that the cross-examiner fears losing a confrontation with the witness and decides to let him get away with it, in the hope that it will not be remembered. However, this is not a real option. Like the Greek philosopher Heraclitus taught, when you step into the stream, it is not the same stream. Once the witness says it, it cannot be unsaid or ignored.

Let's look at a few of the tactics at our disposal using our hypothetical cross-examination.

Impeachment

The easiest way to bring a witness back in line is with a hard piece of evidence, such as a transcript, document, or a video. If the witness deviates from that hard piece of evidence, you then use that evidence as your tool to Pull the Chain.

Q: How sure are you that Mr. A punched Mr. B?

A: I am 100 percent sure.

Q: How far away were you when you made this identification that you're 100 percent sure about?

A: I don't remember how far away, but it was close enough for me to see Mr. A punch Mr. B.

The witness clearly knows where this is going and is trying to minimize the blow before it is even delivered. But he does it to his own detriment because fifty yards is the indisputable distance, and he never saw the puncher's face.

> Q: This is a picture from a security camera showing you at the relevant time standing in front of Lou's Cafe, which is fifty yards away from where Mr. B was punched. Were you standing in front of Lou's cafe fifty yards away when Mr. B was punched?
> A: Yes.

Let's stop there for now. We used a controlled open-ended question to try and get the witness to say the "fifty yards away" answer in his own words, but he avoided the answer because he knows the reference to distance hurts the reliability of his identification. Instead of answering, he claims a lack of specific knowledge and then tries to reinforce his position by assuring, "it was close enough."

An important part of deciding what to do is deciding what *not* to do. The way we dealt with this was not to assert that the witness is a liar, because we can't, given his claimed lack of memory of the distance. While we may think that he is feigning ignorance, it doesn't matter unless we have the goods to demonstrate it.

We also don't try to object and move to strike the second part of the answer as non-responsive. Doing so would be foolish for two reasons: 1) we would likely lose the objection and diminish our credibility; and 2) even if we were successful in having the objection sustained, it wouldn't matter since everyone has already heard the witness say it, and thus the issue needs to be dealt with.

Given all that, we should use the hard evidence to bring the witness back in line by establishing that he was fifty yards away at the time of the identification. As they say, we can take the easy road or the hard road. For the cross-examiner, the hard road is more fruitful since you can leave it littered with the witness's credibility in tatters behind you.

Ask It Again

If the witness avoids answering your question, you ask it again. Not only do you ask it again, but you ask it as close as possible to exactly as you did before. The point is to compel the witness to answer the question under the threat that the trier of fact will see that the witness is nakedly being evasive.

Q: How sure are you that Mr. A punched Mr. B?

A: I am 100 percent sure.

Q: How far away were you when you made this identification that you're 100 percent sure about?

A: I don't remember how far away, but it was close enough for me to see Mr. A punch Mr. B.

Q: This is a picture from a security camera showing you at the relevant time standing in front of Lou's Cafe, which is fifty yards away from where Mr. B was punched. Were you standing in front of Lou's cafe fifty yards away when Mr. B was punched?

A: Well, you got to understand that it was really hot outside that day and the other restaurants were very busy. So I went to Lou's Cafe since the lines aren't very long, and they make really good ice cream.

Q: I didn't ask why you were at Lou's Cafe. I asked if you were in front of Lou's Cafe, fifty yards away from where Mr. B was punched?

A: I guess so.

Q: I'm not asking you to guess. Here is the picture of you standing in front of Lou's Cafe at the time in question. I now ask you for the third time, were you standing in front of Lou's Cafe, fifty yards away from where Mr. B was punched?

A: Yes.

I could keep this up all day. This evading witness comes off as either not credible, a fool, or both. Either way, I'm not the one with the problem. The trier of fact gets to see and hear all of this game playing and, in the end, it's fifty yards no matter what. The witness's duck and cover routine is the sweet cherry on top.

CHAPTER SEVENTEEN
The Rule of Probability

This is perhaps the most important and complex of our techniques, and I have intentionally placed it at the end after laying the foundation for the others. Frankly, this technique goes far beyond any specific method and instead permeates through the entire strategy of cross-examination, as well as the case as a whole. Indeed, this is what we use to evaluate our case when it first comes in, and then we continually reuse it as new information comes in.

Moreover, invocation of the Rule of Probability often leads to the discovery of additional evidence in the pretrial stage. If one claims to have made a telephone call, we know there is evidence to support the claim because there *must* be records. Most of the cases that go to trial do so because there is not clear evidence of who is right and who is wrong. When there is not clear evidence of the "truth," the litigants who most effectively use the Rule of Probability will persuade the trier of fact to vote for their version of the case.

What is this mysterious Rule of Probability? To understand what it is, we must first understand what it is not. The Rule of Probability is not a bright line rule that we can formulaically apply to every situation like others. Impeaching a witness using their previous statements or other evidence is fairly straightforward. If the witness says something in conflict with a piece of evidence, you confront them with it to show that their testimony was inaccurate. The Ask it Again technique is also fairly clear. If someone doesn't answer your question, make them by repeating the question until they do.

The Rule of Probability, on the other hand, is a concept grounded in the principle that reasonable people will agree to certain things based on common sense. For example, I think all reasonable people would agree that it is normal to wear a winter coat and gloves when it is below freezing outside. On the other hand, I think all reasonable people would agree it is not normal to wear a winter coat and gloves in the blazing hot summer.

The thing to understand is that when the cross-examiner makes an assertion and the witness makes a denial, the jurors vote inside their heads whether to agree with the premise of the question or the answer. They do not wait for the end of the cross-examination, much less the end of the case. They vote internally then and there on each question and answer. In voting, they use the material in the case—to be sure—but all that measured against the Rule of Probability, which is another name for plain common sense.

Now these prior examples of coats are easy since they lay in the extreme of their respective positions. But the area between those extremes is where the challenge lies. In order to successfully navigate these waters, we must be able to infer how a trier of fact will vote in their minds on the reasonableness of the issue. And this is exactly what the witness will be doing, as well, in crafting their answers.

Recognizing that this is a bit esoteric, let's dive back into the hypothetical from our last end-point to put this into context (with only one new question in italics at the end):

Q: How sure are you that Mr. A punched Mr. B?

A: I am 100 percent sure.

Q: How far away were you when you made this identification that you're 100 percent sure about?

A: I don't remember how far away, but it was close enough for me to see Mr. A punch Mr. B.

Q: This is a picture from a security camera showing you at the relevant time standing in front of Lou's Cafe, which is fifty yards away from where Mr. B was punched. Were you standing in front of Lou's Cafe fifty yards away when Mr. B was punched?

A: Well, you got to understand that it was really hot outside that day and the other restaurants were very busy. So I went to Lou's Cafe since the lines aren't very long and they make really good ice cream.

Q: I didn't ask why you were at Lou's Cafe. I asked if you were in front of Lou's Cafe, fifty yards away from where Mr. B was punched?

A: I guess so.

Q: I'm not asking you to guess. Here is the picture of you standing in front of Lou's Cafe at the time in question. I now ask you for the third time, were you standing in front of Lou's Cafe, fifty yards away from where Mr. B was punched?

A: Yes.

Q: From your view fifty yards away, what did the assailant's face look like when he punched Mr. B?

A: Well, I didn't actually see his face. I never saw the front side of his body, but Mr. A's rear profile looks like the person I saw punch Mr. B.

Q: You're 100 percent positive Mr. A punched Mr. B even though you never saw his face and were standing half a football field away at the time?

A: Yes.

Q: *Would you agree that seeing the back of someone's head is not as good as seeing their face?*

Now, what's he going to say? I have no idea. He may admit it is better, he may say it's not, or he may start singing his favorite song. I only know one thing: most reasonable people will agree that seeing someone's face is materially better in identifying them than seeing their back (provided, of course, that there is not something unusual about the person's rear profile). And we can therefore be reasonably certain as to how the trier of fact is answering these questions in their minds as the witness speaks his.

I am using the Rule of Probability to control this witness, and he is doing the same thing in his mind as he decides the answers. He will try to figure out if there is something else he can credibly say to get out of this jam. In the end, he has to decide whether to take his medicine or make a proverbial run for it. Let's suppose he tries to slip out of any definite answer:

A: I think seeing someone's face is generally better, but you know, every circumstance is different.

Clever, isn't it? He has tried to play the even-keeled philosopher by trying to answer the question accurately when
he is, of course, utilizing a tool of evasion. The witness is
using his own Rule of Probability analysis to try and escape
the vise, since all reasonable people would agree that every
circumstance is different. But there is a fatal flaw in his
logic. Try using your own Rule of Probability analysis to
identify it before it is revealed in the next question.

> Q: How is this situation any different from one where
> someone sees the back of another person's head for
> the first time from fifty yards away and never gets
> to see their face?

Now where is he going? He bought an extra chess move
with his previous answer, but I don't think he has another
wiggle left where he can survive with his credibility intact.
The fatal flaw in his logic has been exposed. He did not
previously know the defendant, and the defendant doesn't
have some unique identifying mark or bodily feature on
the back of his body. Now, if that were not the case, the
analysis would be different.

But be careful about going too far. For example, here is
an ill-advised follow-up question:

> Q: Since you never saw the person's face and were fifty
> yards away, it is impossible for you to have made
> an accurate identification, isn't it?

You're (hopefully) cringing, since you can hear the answer
in your own mind. Many would refer to this as an error

born of "asking one question too many." But that is incorrect. There is never one question too many. There are only good questions and bad questions. Good questions control the witness, and bad questions do not. Questions that respect the Rule of Probability and those that do not. Here is the painful answer:

> **Q:** Since you never saw the person's face and were fifty yards away, it is impossible for you to have made an accurate identification, isn't it?
>
> **A:** No. It was a clear day, and I had a good line of sight. The defendant has the same hair color, hair style, and build of the man I saw brutally punch the victim. There is no doubt in my mind that the man seated over there is the man who did it.

This question's use of the word "impossible" was a bridge too far. But why? That single word caused a relaxation of the Rule of Probability and provided the witness an opportunity to inflict punishment on the cross-examiner, because most reasonable people would not agree that it is "impossible" for someone to make an identification via the back of someone at fifty yards away for all of the reasons that the witness unloaded upon us in his answer.

There is no doubt that the word "impossible" was a mistake. But what are the right word(s)? How about "almost impossible," "extremely difficult," "challenging," or "hard?" These are better but remain a difficult decision that can only be resolved by using the Rule of Probability. If you go too high on the bar, the witness can credibly disagree, as he did with "impossible." If you set the bar too low (i.e., slightly problematic), they will too easily clear it and undermine your argument. But, in fact, there was no need for any additional word or even for this question. The cross-examiner had already won, and the Rule of Probability does not support us pressing further. Time to stop!

When we think back to the beginning of this hypothetical, it should become clear that this cross-examination was always going to end up here. This witness is not a liar but will also never admit that he is wrong. The cross-examiner has the tools to demonstrate that the identification conditions supported the possibilities of error and could lead to a mistake. And in the absence of clear evidence, the trier of fact will have to decide which version of events to vote for. And in a situation where the evidence is not clear, the person who best harnesses the power of the Rule of Probability will be most credible.

This is the process we have to engage with on every line of questioning for every witness. Unless you have clear evidence driving the outcome of the case (which means that the case probably won't go to trial), the successful side will be the one with the advocate best able to harness the Rule of Probability in conjunction with the other cross-examination techniques.

PART 2

CHAPTER EIGHTEEN

The People of the State of Alabama vs. William Robert Gambini and Stanley Marcus Rothenstein

W e have covered the strategy and the tactics of how to cross-examine a witness. Then we applied them to a hypothetical cross-examination to see them in context. Now, we will take the next step and apply our strategy and tactics to some "famous" cases. You may already be aware of these cases. If so, I am confident you will see them in a new light after experiencing them through our new lens.

We will go over what is good and what is bad, and show how things could have been done better. It is, of course, always easier to look back on things with the benefit of hindsight, and no one plays the game perfectly. But looking back is an important tool for learning. Sports teams look back by studying the previous game's footage to enhance technique in the quest for future victories.

Here is the background of the first case. In 1992, William R. Gambini and Stanley M. Rothenstein were charged with Murder in the First Degree and Accessory to First Degree Murder for killing Jimmy Willis, the clerk at the Sac-O-Suds convenience store. There were no witnesses to the murder nor any weapon recovered. The prosecution's case relied upon three eyewitnesses who all claimed to have seen the defendants arrive at the store in their 1964 metallic green Buick Skylark convertible; that, minutes after arriving, gunshots were heard; and that the defendants were then seen running from the store moments after the shots were fired, getting into the same car they arrived in.

The defendants, in turn, claimed that while they did go into the store, they did not shoot the Sac-O-Suds clerk. Simply put, if the prosecution is able to prove what the witnesses claim they saw, the case is circumstantially strong enough to secure a conviction. Jim Trotter III represented the prosecution, Vincent Gambini represented his cousin, William R. Gambini, and John Gibbons represented the co-defendant Stanley M. Rothenstein.

Opening Statements

Jim Trotter III on behalf of the People of the State of Alabama:

> Your Honor, Counsel, members of the jury, the evidence in this case is going to show that at 9:30 in the morning, January 4, both defendants, Stanley Rothenstein and William Gambini, were seen getting out of their metallic green 1964 Buick Skylark convertible with a white top. The evidence is gonna show that they were seen entering the Sac-O-Suds convenience store in Wazoo City. The evidence is

going to show that minutes after they entered the Sac-O-Suds, a gunshot was heard by three eyewitnesses. You're gonna then hear the testimony of the three eyewitnesses who saw the defendants running out of the Sac-O-Suds a moment after the shots were heard, getting into their faded, metallic green 1964 Buick Skylark, and driving off in great haste. Finally, the State is going to prove that the defendants, Gambini and Rothenstein, admitted and then recanted their testimony to the Sheriff of Beacham County. Now, let's get down to the live-long. Your verdict is gonna depend on what you think of the sworn testimony. Not what I think. What I think don't count. You're the jury. It's your job to decide who's telling the truth. Truth. That's what verdict means. It's a word that comes down from old England, and all our little old ancestors. Now we're going to be asking you to return a verdict of Murder in the First Degree for William Gambini, and a verdict of Accessory to Murder in the First Degree, for Stanley Rothenstein, for helping Gambini commit this heinous crime.[4]

Vincent Gambini on behalf of William Robert Gambini:

Everything that guy just said is bullshit. Thank you.

John Gibbons on behalf of Stanley Marcus Rothenstein:

Ladies and gentlemen of the jury. On January 4, my client did indeed visit the Sac-O-Suds convenience store. But he didn't kill anyone. He, uh—We intend to prove that the prosecution's case is circumstantial and, and, and, and, and coincidental. Thank you.

Sam Tipton

The prosecution's first witness is Sam Tipton, who testified in relevant part on Direct Examination that:

> A: . . . I heard a gunshot so I looked out the window, and I seen them two boys run out, get into their car, and drive off like maniacs, tire smoking screeching, going up on the curb.
>
> Q: Is this the car?
>
> A: Yes, sir.

While not an eyewitness to the actual murder, Mr. Tipton's testimony is devastating to the defense. He places the defendants and their car at the scene of the crime, has them in the store when the shot is fired, and then has them fleeing the scene just after the gunshot is fired. Let's analyze two cross-examinations of the same witness. First, we have Mr. Gibbons on behalf of Defendant Rothenstein:

> Q: Mr. Tipton. Now, when you viewed my client, how far away were you?
>
> A: About fifty feet.

This first question warns of the likely failure of this cross-examination since it reveals that Mr. Gibbons does not possess a structurally sound plan. The problem is not, however, the open ended question. A leading question would cause the same result. The real problem is that Mr. Gibbons's strategy for demonstrating the inaccuracy of the testimony is unsound because the evidence and the Rule of Probability don't support it.

Unlike our own hypothetical, the issue with Mr. Tipton is not the distance he was from the people he claims to be able to identify. But why? The defendants must admit that they were in the store because they purchased items from the store and, in fact, they do eventually admit that they went there. As such, whatever distance Mr. Tipton was at, he was at least able to accurately identify the defendants when they entered the store.

> Q: Oh, now do you think that's close enough to make an accurate identification?
> A: Yes.

Things have gotten worse for Mr. Gibbons since the incorrect strategy has driven him into this painful and completely foreseeable brick wall. Neither Mr. Tipton, nor any witness on cross-examination, is going to simply recant what they previously said on direct-examination unless the evidence or the Rule of Probability forces them do so.

Again, the form of the question doesn't matter because a leading question would have resulted in the same outcome. For example, if a leading question was asked instead—"Fifty feet is not close enough to make an accurate identification, is it?"—the answer would still have been "Yes, it is." Or even worse, it would have been "Yes, it is. That's the same distance I saw them from when they went into the store."

The defense simply does not have the evidence or the power pursuant to the Rule of Probability to make this a successful line of attack. Mr. Tipton is always going to say that he was able to make an accurate identification from fifty feet away and the defense will have to agree that he was at least correct in identifying the defendants entering the store.

> Q: Mr. Tipton, I see you wear eyeglasses.
> A: Sometimes.
> Q: Well, would you care to show these eyeglasses to the jury please?
> Q: Thank you. Now, Mr. Tipton, were you wearing them that day?
> A: No.

Some might be tempted to think that Mr. Gibbons has now secured a successful victory with these two questions, but that is incorrect. This issue reminds me again of the film *White Men Can't Jump*. This time it is Rosie Perez's character explaining to Woody Harrelson's character that "Sometimes when you win, you really lose . . . "[5] Indeed, this is the kind of fake victory that crushes an advocate and their client in the end, since the brief moment of elevation only makes the fall occur from a greater height.

Not only has Mr. Gibbons failed to pursue the correct strategy from the outset, but his inevitable failure to get Mr. Tipton to admit that he couldn't make an accurate identification has propelled him to reach into an even more dangerous line of questioning about the quality of his vision. Refusing to give up on the previously bad line of questioning, Mr. Gibbons doubles down and asks a question to which he does not know the answer in the hope of salvaging an already unsuccessful cross-examination.

Mr. Tipton's answer that he sometimes wears eyeglasses and wasn't wearing them that day appears at first blush to bolster Mr. Gibbons's theory. Some would argue that he should take this victory and sit down. But this is not an example of asking one too many questions or going too far. Remember, there are only good questions and bad questions. The die is now cast whether Mr. Gibbons asks the next question or not, because the prosecution will bring it out on re-direct.

Q: You see, you were fifty feet away, you made a positive eyewitness identification, and yet you were not wearing your necessary prescription eyeglasses.

A: They're reading glasses.

Q: Could you tell the Court what color eyes the defendants have?

A: Brown. Hazel green.

Q: No more questions.

Six questions is all it took for Mr. Gibbons to destroy his own credibility and convict his client because he did not have a sound strategy for the witness, did not understand the evidence, and did not respect the Rule of Probability. As such, this cross-examination never could have been successful and only supported the prosecution's case.

Now let's take a look at Mr. Tipton's subsequent cross-examination by Mr. Vincent Gambini on behalf of Defendant William Gambini:

Q: Mr. Tipton, when you viewed the defendants walking from their car into the Sac-O-Suds, what angle was your point of view?
A: They was kinda walking toward me when they entered the store.
Q: And when they left, what angle was your point of view?
A: They was kinda walking away from me.

Unlike Mr. Gibbons, Mr. Gambini has correctly identified a fertile line of questioning. Instead of focusing on the distance, Mr. Gambini is focused on the angle of Mr. Tipton's view since he knows that he must concede that Mr. Tipton saw the defendants enter the store. Mr. Gambini's use of a controlled open-ended question (that he knows the answer to) makes it all the better since it forces the witness to admit in his own words that he had a frontal (better) view of them upon entering, but a rear (worse) view of them leaving.

Q: Would you say you got a better shot of them going in, but not so much coming out?
A: You could say that.
Q: I did say that. Would you say that?
A: Yeah.

Using another controlled opened-ended question, Mr. Gambini not only elicited more persuasive testimony from the witness than a simple yes or no, but he has frustrated

Mr. Tipton, who sees that the accuracy of his identification is being diminished, but is nevertheless powerless to stop it because the Rule of Probability has forced him to comply.

Because most reasonable people would agree that seeing someone from the front is better than from behind, Mr. Gambini is in no danger and can instead force Mr. Tipton to choose between two bad choices: admit the fact or make things worse by being evasive. Mr. Tipton (as many witness do) tries to evade giving a damaging answer by saying "You could say that," which is not answering the question.

Mr. Tipton has attempted to cheat, but it is up to Mr. Gambini to make him pay for it.

Attorneys will too often stop here because they do not want to risk diminishing their victory or they simply didn't hear the witness's answer. But this is far from the time to let up. Instead, this is the time to Pull the Chain and damage Mr. Tipton's credibility by asking him the question again and forcing him to answer it.

This is gold for the defense. By putting this pressure on Mr. Tipton, Mr. Gambini has scored a double victory: he has diminished Mr. Tipton's credibility while also bolstering his theory of the case.

Q: Is it possible the two youths who entered the store were not the same youths you saw leaving the store?
A: No. Why would they get into the same car?

Mr. Gambini has now stated, in the form of a question, the defense's theory of the case: That while the defendants did enter the store, they were not the same men who left after the shot was fired. But he errs in not making the entire theory clear, which provides Mr. Tipton an opportunity to seek revenge by pointing out the glaring hole in the defense's theory: that a different group of people wouldn't leave in the same car as the one the defendants drove up in.

I often refer to this as "moving in for the kill too soon." In order to make this point more credible, Mr. Gambini cannot haphazardly rush to the end and expect the witness to fall over. Instead, like Frank Sinatra said, we must make all of the stops along the way.

> Q: Let me re-phrase the question. Is it possible that the two defendants entered the store, picked out twenty-two specific items off the shelves, heated up a burrito, had the clerk pour a slush drink, take money, make change then leave, then, two different men drive up in a *similar looking* car, go in, tie up the clerk, rob him, shoot him, and leave? [Emphasis added].
>
> A: No. They didn't have enough time.

Mr. Tipton's previous answer hurt because Mr. Gambini's hasty question did not clearly articulate the defense's theory. Mr. Gambini fortunately recognizes his mistake and recovers well through his "re-phrase" of the question. But don't be fooled: this is anything but a simple "re-phrase" and instead a critically important repositioning of the entire cross-examination toward the issue that matters—time. That is why Mr. Gambini adds the critically important facts of how many things the defendants did in the store—to elongate the amount of time that had to have passed between when they arrived and when they left.

> **Q:** How much time were they in the store?
> **A:** Five minutes.

Mr. Gambini masterfully uses a controlled open-ended question utilizing the Rule of Probability and no answer can hurt him. If Mr. Tipton chooses a short amount of time (as he likely would, given his previous answer), then Mr. Gambini has the upper hand since the defendants' numerous actions in the store make five minutes seem unreasonably short and thus diminish Mr. Tipton's credibility. If Mr. Tipton chose a longer period of time, it supports the defense's theory that there was enough time for a different group of men to arrive in a similar looking car and commit the crime after the defendants left the store.

> **Q:** Are you sure it was five minutes? Did you look at your watch?
> **A:** No.

Mr. Gambini's question(s) here, while not fatal, could be improved. He asked two different questions, which resulted in a lack of clarity to which query the "No" answer is responding.

> **Q:** Oh, oh, I'm sorry, you testified earlier that the boys went into the store and you had just begun to make breakfast, you were just ready to eat and you heard

> a gunshot, so obviously it takes you five minutes to make breakfast?
>
> A: That's right.
>
> Q: So you knew that. Do you remember what you had?
>
> A: Eggs and grits.

Mr. Gambini's original question was poorly constructed and did not elicit the answer he wanted. His follow-up question now finely draws its point and uses the witness's previous testimony to lock him into position. Mr. Gambini's seemingly simple question about what Mr. Tipton had for breakfast is the key to discrediting this witness's testimony through the Limiting technique and by using the organization of the questions to put the witness into a box.

> Q: How do you make your grits? Regular, creamy, or al dente?
>
> A: Uh, just regular, I guess.
>
> Q: Instant grits?
>
> A: No self-respecting southerner uses instant grits. I take pride in my grits.

These two questions are both designed to limit Mr. Tipton's ability to shrink the amount of time the defendants were in the store. While not problematic, doing this as one question would be easily accomplished and therefore preferable.

> Q: So Mr. Tipton, how could it take you only five minutes to cook your grits—when it takes the entire grit-eating world twenty minutes?
>
> A: I dunno, I'm a fast cook, I guess.

Mr. Gambini's hard work has paid off, and he has moved in for the kill. He has established that Mr. Tipton was incorrect about how much time had passed, which gives life to the defense's theory that there was time for two other men to enter the store and kill the clerk. But if that wasn't good enough, Mr. Tipton has made this all the sweeter by refusing to admit what everyone listening already knows. This thus presents another opportunity to attack Mr. Tipton's credibility by repeating the question and forcing him to answer.

> Q: A fast cook? That's it? Are we to believe that boiling water soaks into a grit quicker in your kitchen than any other place on the face of the earth?
>
> A: I dunno.
>
> Q: Perhaps the laws of physics cease to exist on your stove? Were these "magic grits"? Did you buy them from the guy who sold Jack his beanstalk beans? You sure about that five minutes?
>
> A: I . . . may have been mistaken.

Recognizing that this witness did not need to be a liar to be wrong, Mr. Gambini has masterfully damaged Mr. Tipton's credibility by using controlled open-ended questions utilizing the Credibility Attack and Limiting techniques. As a result, any previous doubt that the defendants could have "picked out twenty-two specific items off the shelves, heated up a burrito, had the clerk pour a slush drink, take money, make change then leave" in *five minutes* has been extinguished.

Let's discuss Mr. Gambini's order and organization of this cross-examination. He had two essential points to make: 1) that the identification of the defendants leaving the store was unreliable due to the viewpoint; and 2) that enough time passed between when the defendants came into the store and when the shot was fired for two other men to have arrived and shot the clerk.

Could Mr. Gambini's organization have been different? I think he could have done it in the opposite order and it still would have been effective, but the order that he chose makes the most sense with all else being equal, since it is a linear dismantling of what happened. In the end, the decision does not rest on some primacy/recency theory, but rather on welding the order of the questions to make the most persuasive argument.

Notice how Mr. Gambini uses the sequence of his questions to limit the witness. For example, if he doesn't establish that the witness was eating grits, then that whole line of questioning would fall apart because it would be possible to eat other kinds of breakfast in five minutes.

Mr. Gambini's work has not won the case, but at least it has saved the defense from certain destruction following Mr. Gibbons's suicidal cross-examination of the witness.

Ernie Crane

The prosecution's second witness was Ernie Crane, who testified in relevant part on Direct Examination that:

Q: Then you saw those two boys run out of the Sac-O-Suds, jump into this car, and drive off?
A: Yeah. They peeled away, car was all over the road.

Like Mr. Tipton, Mr. Crane is not an eyewitness to the murder. But his testimony has the defendants rapidly fleeing the scene of the murder, which gives credibility to the theory that the defendants shot the clerk. After Mr. Gibbons's cross-examination of Mr. Tipton, defendant Rothenstein (wisely) terminated Mr. Gibbons as counsel and retained Mr. Gambini, who now represents both defendants. Mr. Gambini begins the cross-examination by using photographs with his questions.

> Q: Mr. Crane, what're these of?
> A: My house and stuff.
> Q: What's this brown stuff on your window?
> A: Dirt.
> Q: What is this . . . rusty, dusty, dirty-looking thing on your window?
> A: It's a screen.

Mr. Gambini utilizes three controlled open-ended questions to establish that there is a lot of dirt and a rusty screen on Mr. Crane's house's window. This works well since it forces the witness to answer in his own words without appearing to be controlled. But he is, of course, being controlled since the answers to the questions are controlled by the photographs. As the next question demonstrates, however, Mr. Gambini's questions could have been asked more persuasively.

> Q: What're all these really big things right in the middle of your view from the window of your kitchen and the Sac-O-Suds? What would you call these things?
> A: Trees.

Notice that Mr. Gambini's question structure has changed (for the better). It is still a controlled open-ended question, but he has added the material part about the object being "right in the middle of your view from the window of your kitchen and the Sac-O-Suds." This is the most material part of the question, and it should have been layered into each of the preceding questions to make them more persuasive. This last question makes clear that Mr. Gambini's strategy is to utilize the Credibility Attack and Limiting techniques to demonstrate that Mr. Crane was not actually able to see what he claims to have seen, given the many obstructions blocking his view.

> **Q:** What do you call these thousands of little things on the trees?
> **A:** Leaves.
> **Q:** And these . . . "bushy" things between the trees. What do you call these?
> **A:** Bushes.

Again, Mr. Gambini misses the opportunity to interweave the central issue into his questions. While not fatal, it would make the questions even more persuasive, and there is no downside. Compare the choice for yourself: "What do you call these thousands of little things on the trees?" or "What do you call these thousands of little things on the trees that were right in the middle of your view from the window of your kitchen and the Sac-O-Suds?"

> **Q:** So, you can positively identify the defendants, at a distance of eighty feet, for a moment of two

seconds, looking through this dirty window, this
crud-covered screen, these trees with these leaves
on them and through . . . how many bushes?

A: Looks like five.

Mr. Gambini's primary question does two excellent things.
First, it utilizes the looping method to reincorporate all
of Mr. Crane's previous answers to make the obstructed
view argument even more persuasive. Second, it incorpo-
rates new facts which have not yet been elicited, that the
distance was eighty feet and the amount of time was two
seconds. Both of these numbers strengthen Mr. Gambini's
cross-examination argument that Mr. Crane was not in
a position to make an accurate identification. All true
because of the power of the Rule of Probability.

However, Mr. Gambini realized mid-question that
he made a mistake—he forget to elicit how many bushes
were obstructing Mr. Crane's view. Now this was a
mistake because Mr. Gambini was asking a very good
question, and it was probably not worth abandoning it
to cover how many bushes there were. But Mr. Gambini
gets lucky because Mr. Crane makes an even bigger mistake in minimizing the number of bushes. This provides
Mr. Gambini a new opportunity to diminish Mr. Crane's
credibility.

Q: Don't forget this one and this one.
A: Seven bushes.

Instead of this being a distraction from his earlier question, it ends up being fortuitous. Sometimes we get lucky

in making a mistake that turns out well. Nevertheless, the job here is to call it straight, warts and all.

> Q: Seven bushes. So whattya think? Is it possible you just saw two guys in a green convertible, but not necessarily these particular two guys?
>
> A: I suppose.

Notice how this question differs from the previous one where he asked, "So, you can positively identify the defendants . . . " Instead of asking this, he changes tactics and uses the question as an opportunity to further advance his theory of the case: that the people who committed the crime were two different men in a similar looking car.

Mr. Crane's "I suppose" response is the best he can muster because any other answer will not be credible, since everyone listening has already heard the answer in their own head. Now some may be thinking that this "I suppose" answer is evasive and thus an opportunity to Pull the Chain. Doing so, however, would likely be a mistake since the premise of the question was "Is it possible . . . "

This language is the most that the Rule of Probability will permit. If Mr. Gambini had said something like "certainly" or "definitely," then the witness would have room to disagree under the Rule of Probability because the evidence only went so far as to cast doubt on the reliability of the identification, not to definitively prove it was someone else. In any event, the effectiveness of the witness's identification has been *limited*—right out of the case.

Constance Riley

The prosecution's third witness was Constance Riley, who testified in relevant part on Direct Examination that:

A: Then I heard two loud "bangs" like firecrackers. I looked up and saw two young men run out from the Sac-O-Suds, jump into a green car with a white convertible top, and drive off like the dickens, tires spinning.

Q: Mrs. Riley, are those two young men present in the courtroom today?

A: Yes, they are.

Q: Can you point them out for me?

A: They're sitting right there.

Q: Is this the car?

A: Yes, it is.

Q: Let the record show that Constance Riley identified the defendant's car.

Like Mr. Tipton and Mr. Crane, Mrs. Riley is not an eyewitness to the murder. But her testimony has the defendants fleeing the scene of the murder right after the shots were fired and then driving away in their car, supporting the theory that the defendants shot the clerk. Mr. Gambini cross-examines on behalf of both defendants.

Q: Mrs. Riley, were you wearing your glasses when you viewed the defendants?

A: Yes, I was.

Mr. Gambini's plan is to challenge the quality of Mrs. Riley's vision to undermine her identification testimony. It is worth asking: how is this different from Mr. Gibbons's ill-advised eyeglasses gambit with Mr. Tipton? We shall see if it is.

> Q: Can you put them on? Whoa! How long you been wearing glasses?
>
> A: Since I was six.
>
> Q: Were they as thick as these?
>
> A: Oh, no. They got thicker over the years.
>
> Q: So, as your eyes have gotten more and more out of whack as you've gotten older, how many different levels of thickness have you gone through?
>
> A: Oh, I don't know, over forty years, probably ten times.
>
> Q: So, you've gotten new glasses around every four years. How long you been wearing this level of thickness?
>
> A: About four years.
>
> Q: Maybe you're due for a thicker set?
>
> A: Oh no, I think they're okay.

So, Mrs. Riley is elderly and her glasses are very thick. Mr. Gambini's controlled open-ended questions elicit the favorable testimony that Mrs. Riley's eyes have had issues since she was six years old, that she usually gets new glasses every four years, and that it has been four years since she got new glasses. Notwithstanding this favorable testimony, Mrs. Riley stands fast and does not say what Mr. Gambini wants to hear—that she needs new glasses—which would

Limit the reliability of her identification of the defendants and their vehicle.

Mr. Gambini now has a decision to make: does he stop here with what he has elicited and rely upon the Rule of Probability to argue that her identification is unreliable because she is at the end of her four-year cycle? Or does he take a significant risk and press forward in the hope of achieving more, but also potentially losing what he has gained?

> Q: Let's be sure. Let's check 'em out. How far away were the defendants from you when you saw them enter the Sac-O-Suds?
>
> A: About a hundred feet.
>
> Q: Okay. Hold this tape measure. This is fifty feet. Half the distance. Ms. Riley, can you see how many fingers I have showing?
>
> J:* Let the record show that counsel is holding up two fingers.
>
> Q: Your Honor, please.
>
> J: I'm sorry.
>
> Q: Now Mrs. Riley, and only Mrs. Riley. How many fingers can you see?
>
> A: Four.
>
> Q: What're you thinking, Mrs. Riley?
>
> A: I'm thinking of getting thicker glasses.

Mr. Gambini has chosen the risky path and fortunately it has paid off. Mrs. Riley was unable to accurately describe

---

* For all following chapters, the letter J will designate when the judge of the trial is speaking in all cross-examination transcripts.

the two fingers that Mr. Gambini was holding up for all to see, and she gracefully acknowledges that her identification is unreliable.

However, just because this gambit worked doesn't mean it was the right move to make. Reasonable people may differ, but for me, this was too much of a risk to take given the circumstantial nature of the prosecution's case, that the previous two witnesses were already discredited, and that this is a capital murder case. Let's examine why.

First, Mr. Gambini gave her the opportunity to view him from fifty feet instead of the one hundred feet identification distance. Second, if Mrs. Riley was able to pass Mr. Gambini's test at fifty feet or even at a hundred feet, it would have significantly bolstered her credibility and cost his credibility dearly.

Given that the two other eyewitness identifications had already been undermined, and since Mrs. Riley testified that she needs glasses to see, that she usually gets a new pair every four years, and that it had been four years since she last got new glasses, there is a strong argument under the Rule of Probability that her identification was also unreliable.

Mr. Gambini should have sat down and not performed an experiment which he could not be sure would have a good outcome. Any doubt about that should be resolved by recalling what happened when the prosecutor's experimented with having O. J. Simpson try on the glove before the jury. Their disastrous experiment was lethal to their case and their standing with the jury. In sum, Mr. Gambini's ill-advised gambit is analogous to a basketball coach telling a player, "great shot, don't do it again."

George Wilbur

The prosecution's case has been severely damaged by Mr. Gambini's cross-examinations. They have no eye-witness to the murder, no murder weapon, and the three witnesses' identifications of the defendants fleeing the store right after the shots were fired have been discredited on cross-examination. If the prosecution now rests, they stand to lose.

Understanding this, the prosecution attempts to salvage its case by calling George Wilbur to the stand even though he is not on their witness list. The judge allows his testimony over Mr. Gambini's objection. Mr. Trotter performs the direct examination on behalf of the prosecution.

Q: Mr. Wilbur, what is your profession?

A: I'm a special automotive instructor of forensic studies for the Federal Bureau of Investigation.

Q: How long have you been working in that position?

A: Eighteen years.

Q: These are photographs of the tires belonging to the defendants' car. And these are photographs of tire marks made by the assailants' car as it fled the Sac-O-Suds convenience store. Are you familiar with these?

A: Yes, I am.

Q: Can you elaborate please?

A: We compared the tire marks outside the convenience store with the rear tires of the defendants' car. They are the same model and size tire, Michelin model XGV, size 75r, fourteen-inch wheel.

Q: They're both the same size and model tire. Anything else, sir?

A: Yes, indeed. The car leaving the convenience store spun its rear tires dramatically, and left a residue of rubber on the asphalt. I took a sample of that rubber and analyzed it. I also took a sample of rubber from the rear tires of the defendants' Buick and analyzed that too.

Q: What kind of equipment did you use to find this out?

A: I used a Hewlett-Packard 5710-A dual-column gas chromatograph with flame analyzation detectors.

Q: Uh-huh. Is that thing turbo-charged?

A: Only on the floor models.

Q: Now, Mr. Wilbur, what was the result of your analysis?

A: The chemical composition between the two tires was found to be identical.

Q: Identical. No more questions.

The prosecution has recovered well considering Mr. Gambini's effective cross-examinations, since they now at least have some physical evidence to bolster their argument. Mr. Gambini cross-examines on behalf of both defendants.

Q: Is it possible that two separate cars could be driving on Michelin model XGV 75R 14s?

A: Of course.

This is a masterful controlled opened-ended question because it forces Mr. Wilbur to put his own stamp on the answer. Imagine instead if Mr. Gambini asked the leading question, "Isn't it true that two separate cars could be driving on Michelin model XGV 75Rs?" And the answer was "yes." Certainly not bad, but not as good as Mr. Wilbur's emphatic "Of course." So why is it better for Mr. Gambini to use a controlled open-ended question here?

Because it looks like Mr. Gambini is not controlling Mr. Wilbur, and it forces Mr. Wilbur to make a choice whether to evade answering a question he does not like or taking his medicine. As we previously saw with Mr. Tipton, good things can happen when we allow a witness the opportunity to hurt themselves when they can do you no harm. Now, Mr. Wilbur is not Mr. Tipton. He is a much more sophisticated witness.

However, he chooses to answer "Of course" instead of simply saying "it is possible" or "sure." But why did he make this choice? While we can never be certain, my view is that Mr. Wilbur understands that his credibility is on the line with every word he says, and he is trying to protect that credibility so much that his instinct is to over-compensate in the other direction since he knows where Mr. Gambini's cross-examination is going.

> Q: Let me ask you this—what is the bestselling, single model tire sold in the United States?
> A: The Michelin XGV.
> Q: And what is the most popular size?
> A: 75R 14.

These next two questions and answers lend significant support to my thesis. Mr. Wilbur knows that this model tire and its size are the bestselling make and model tire sold in the United States, so it certainly is not unlikely that two different cars could have them; it is even probable. Mr.

Gambini's controlled open-ended questions are masterful in forcing Mr. Wilbur to say the make and model himself rather than simply uttering yes to a leading question.

> Q: The same size as the defendants' car?
> A: But two faded green 1964 Buick Skylark convertibles . . . ?

Mr. Wilbur was playing nice for a while and then the rubber hit the road (so to speak). Instead of simply answering the question as he must, Mr. Wilbur suddenly leaps out of his role as the clinical investigator analyzing the data and into a member of the prosecutor's team, bent on securing a conviction.

> Q: I asked if the most popular size of the most popular tire is on the defendants' car.
> A: Well, yeah.
> Q: Thank you. No further questions.

Mr. Gambini wisely punishes him by demonstrating that the witness has exceeded the scope of the question, which demonstrates the witness's bias to the jury. But Mr. Gambini makes a serious mistake in stopping there. Mr. Wilbur did not previously answer his question so he wisely Pulled the Chain, re-asked the question, and forced him to answer. This was valuable to Mr. Gambini because it both bolsters his argument that the marks could have been left by a different car with the same make and model tires, while also diminishing Mr. Wilbur's credibility for refusing to answer his question.

But Mr. Gambini makes the significant mistake of not dealing with the substance of the witness's advocacy as well as its evasion. Mr. Wilbur gave him a gold-plated gift in evading the question about the tire size when he instead answered, "But two faded green 1964 Buick Skylark convertibles . . . ?" Think about it: Where did this statement come from and what should be done with it?

The one thing that should not be done is ignore it like Mr. Gambini did. Instead, this answer should have been turned into a weapon to destroy the credibility of Mr. Wilbur and the advocate who called him to the stand. But how? I would propose something like this with the answers that any rational person would be forced to make (and the answers that everyone would hear nevertheless):

Q: *Now I asked you before if the most popular size tire in the United States, the 75R– 14, was the same size as what was on the defendants' car, didn't I?*

A: *Yes.*

Q: *And you didn't directly answer my question, did you?*

A: *No.*

Q: *Instead of answering my question, you chose to exclaim, "But two faded green 1964 Buick Skylark convertibles . . . ?"*

A: *Yes.*

Q: *Now, your testimony on direct examination was that the only evidence you had were tire marks outside the Sac-O-Suds that were Michelin XGV 75R 14s, which happen to be on the defendants' car along with millions of other vehicles?*

A: *Yes.*

Q: *Where is the physical evidence that these tire marks were caused by a faded green 1964 Buick Skylark convertible as you claimed?*

A: *[Nothing good to say]*

Now you may say that Mr. Wilbur wouldn't have answered the questions this way, and maybe he wouldn't have. I would certainly hope that he would continue trying to evade, creating more and more material for me to diminish his credibility. It may seem counter-intuitive, but these are not straw man answers designed to make him fail, but instead are the best choice available given the formation of the questions and the situation he is in.

Notice that I have chosen to use leading questions except for the last one. I have used the leading method because the substance of the question is what drives the witness in this situation into the corner. In directly going after his credibility, I am not interested in his explanations or what he is thinking, but only in making it clear what he has said doesn't make any sense. The last question is the lone controlled open-ended question to allow Mr. Wilbur the opportunity to explain himself, knowing full well that he has nothing good to say since the truth is that he has no evidence to support the claim and only said it because he was worried the defendants wouldn't be convicted.

In any event, Mr. Wilbur was the last witness for the prosecution. The torch now passes to the defense.

Mona Lisa Vito

While under no obligation to call any witnesses since they have no burden of proof (unlike the prosecution), the defense nevertheless decided to present additional evidence even though Mr. Gambini's cross-examinations severely damaged the prosecution's case. The defense's first witness was Mona Lisa Vito.

Q: [Gambini] Your Honor, the defense calls as its first witness Miss Mona Lisa Vito.

Q: [Trotter] I object, your Honor; this person's not on the witness list.

Q: [Gambini] This witness is an expert in the field of automobiles, and is being called to rebut the testimony of George Wilbur. Miss Vito, you're supposed to be some kind of expert in automobiles, is that correct? Is that correct?

J: Will you please answer the counselor's question?

A: [Vito] No, I hate him.

Q: [Gambini] May I have permission to treat Miss Vito as a hostile witness?

A: [Vito] You think I'm hostile now, wait till you see me tonight.

J: Do you two know each other?

Q: [Gambini] Yeah, she's my fiancéé.

J: Well, that would certainly explain the hostility.

Q: [Trotter] Your Honor, I object to this witness. Improper foundation. I'm not aware of this person's qualifications. I'd like to voir dire this witness as to the extent of her expertise.

J: Granted. Mr. Trotter, you may proceed.

Q: [Trotter] Miss Vito, what's your current profession?

A: [Vito] I'm an out-of-work hairdresser.

Q: [Trotter] Out-of-work hairdresser? Now, in what way does that qualify you as an expert in automobiles?

A: [Vito] It doesn't.

Q: [Trotter] In what way are you qualified?

A: [Vito] Well, my father was a mechanic, his father was a mechanic, my mother's father was a mechanic, my three brothers are mechanics, four uncles on my father's side are mechanics—

Q: [Trotter] Your family is obviously qualified, but have you ever worked as a mechanic?

A: [Vito] Yeah, in my father's garage, yeah.

Q: [Trotter] As a mechanic? What did you do in your father's garage?

A: [Vito] Tune-ups, oil changes, brake relining, engine rebuilds, rebuild some trannies, rear end—

Q: [Trotter] Okay, okay. But does being an ex-mechanic necessarily qualify you as being an expert on tire marks?

A: [Vito] No, thank you, goodbye.

J: Sit down and stay there until you're told to leave.

Q: [Gambini] Your Honor, Miss Vito's expertise is in general automotive knowledge. It is in this area that her testimony will be applicable. Now, if Mr. Trotter wishes to voir dire the witness, I'm sure he's going to be more than satisfied.

J: Okay.

Q: [Trotter] All right, all right. Now, Miss Vito, being an expert on general automotive knowledge, can you tell me what would the correct ignition timing be on a 1955 Bel-Air Chevrolet with a 327 cubic inch engine and a four-barrel carburetor?

A: [Vito] It's a bullshit question.

Q: [Trotter] Does that mean that you can't answer it?

A: [Vito] It's a bullshit question; it's impossible to answer.

Q: [Trotter] Impossible because you don't have the answer.

A: [Vito] Nobody could answer that question.

Q: [Trotter] Your honor, I move to disqualify Miss Vito as an expert witness.

J: Can you answer the question?

A: [Vito] No, it is a trick question.

J: Why is it a trick question?

A: [Vito] Cause Chevy didn't make a 327 in '55. The 327 didn't come out till '62, and it wasn't offered in a Bel-Air with a four-barrel carb 'til '64. However, in 1964 the correct ignition timing would be four degrees before top dead center.

Q: [Trotter] Well, uh, she's acceptable your honor.

Sometimes you can do everything right and still lose. And that's OK as long as you make the most of the hand you're dealt. Let's put aside the procedural issues that the expert witness designation requires and instead focus on Mr. Trotter's questions. This was certainly not a traditional cross-examination, and Mr. Trotter did not have advance notice to prepare. Given all of that, he did a fine job in pressing the credentials of the witness to determine whether she was someone with the appropriate knowledge and background to be deemed an expert.

Given the witness's deep background in general automotive knowledge, demonstrating that she was not an expert in the field was simply a bridge too far. Now, to be fair, Mr. Trotter didn't know that before questioning her so no credibility loss should be attributed to him for that.

But asking a "question" that asserted a factual misrepresentation is a no-no. The witness's ability to show that the cross-examiner was not playing it straight was an unforced credibility error by Mr. Trotter. As we have said and will keep saying, credibility is the coin of the realm, and it should not be gambled or given away.

Q: Your Honor, this is a picture taken by my fiancée outside the Sac-O-Suds. Do we agree on this?

Q: [Trotter] Yeah.

Q: Thank you. I'd like to submit this picture of the tire tracks as evidence.

J: Mr. Trotter?

Q: [Trotter] No objection, your Honor.

Q: Miss Vito, did you take this picture?

A: You know I did.

Q: And what is this picture of?

A: You know what it's of. [It's a picture of dog poop in between a set of tire tracks.]

Q: Miss Vito, it has been argued by me, the defense, that two sets of guys met up at the Sac-O-Suds at the same time, driving identical metallic mint green 1964 Buick Skylark convertibles. Now, can you tell us, by looking at the picture, if the defense's case holds water? [pause] Miss Vito, please answer the question. Does the defense's case hold water?

This question is simply confounding and deserves exploration given the earlier commentary about Mr. Wilbur's cross-examination. The record is completely devoid of the defense ever making the argument that the other car had to be the same year, make, and model as the defendants' car. Not only did Mr. Gambini never make this argument, but he made a different (and correct) argument on the cross-examination of Mr. Tipton which is reproduced below:

> Q: Let me re-phrase the question. Is it possible that the two defendants entered the store, picked out twenty-two specific items off the shelves, heated up a burrito, had the clerk pour a slush drink, take money, make change then leave, then, two different men drive up in a *similar-looking car*, go in, tie up the clerk, rob him, shoot him, and leave? [Emphasis added.]

Instead, the idea of two identical cars was only first mentioned by George Wilbur on cross-examination in response to a different question. As such, it appears that Mr. Gambini has allowed Mr. Wilbur to affect his own theory of the case. Whatever the reason, we cannot let this strategy mistake go unanswered.

Mr. Gambini is, however, not going to be hurt by this because this is now a straw man argument for Miss Vito to swiftly knock down. But the lack of negative consequence in this particular situation does not change the fact that this was the wrong theory of defense instead of the two similar-looking men in a similar-looking car defense. And it was this point that Mr. Gambini did not take advantage of on Mr. Wilbur's cross-examination (before he figured out Miss Vito's importance to the case).

The facts and the Rule of Probability strongly support the argument that there are many similar-looking cars with the same kind of tires in the world. That Mr. Gambini belatedly realized that Miss Vito had physical proof excluding the defendants from committing the crime is a red-herring for our own learning and analysis. What if Mr. Gambini didn't belatedly figure it out, what if Miss Vito wasn't allowed to testify, and so on. Remember, no one does it perfectly. But we all do better with practice, particularly if it is critiqued with disciplined honesty.

A: No, the defense is wrong.

Q: Are you sure?

A: I'm positive.

Q: How could you be so sure?

A: Because there is no way that these tire marks were made by a 1964 Buick Skylark. These marks were made by a 1963 Pontiac Tempest.

Q: [Trotter] Objection, your Honor, can we clarify to the court whether the witness is stating fact or opinion?

J: This is your opinion?

A: It's a fact.

Q: I find it hard to believe that this kind of information could be ascertained simply by looking at a picture.

A: Would you like me to explain?

Q: I would love to hear this.

J: So would I.

A: The car that made these two equal length tire marks had positraction, can't make those marks without positraction, which is not available on the 1964 Buick Skylark.

Q: And why not? What is positraction?

A: It's a limited slip deferential which distributes power equally to both the right and left tires. The '64 Skylark had a regular deferential, which anyone who's been stuck in the mud in Alabama knows, you step on the gas, one tire spins, the other tire does nothing.

Q: Is that it?

A: No, there's more; you see, when the left tire mark goes up on the curb, and the right tire mark stays flat and even, well, the '64 Skylark had a solid rear axle, so when the left tire would go up on the curb, the right tire would tilt out and ride along its edge, but that didn't happen here, the tire marks stayed flat and even. This car had an independent rear suspension. Now in the sixties there were only two other cars made in America that had positraction and independent rear suspension and enough power to make these marks. One was the Corvette, which could never be confused with the Buick Skylark. The other had the same body length, height, width, weight, wheel-base, and wheel-track as the '64 Skylark, and that was the 1963 Pontiac Tempest.

Q: And because both cars were made by GM, were both cars available in metallic mint green paint?

A: They were.

> Q: Thank you, Miss Vito, no more questions. Thank you very, very much. You've been a lovely, lovely witness.
>
> J: Mr. Trotter, would you like to question Miss Vito?
>
> Q: [Trotter] No further questions.

While this is not technically a cross-examination (since Mr. Gambini's request to treat the witness as hostile was never ruled on by the judge), it doesn't matter. Treating a witness on direct as hostile only provides the ability to use leading questions. But that doesn't matter when we have mastered the use of controlled open-ended questions like Mr. Gambini. Look back at his questions. He is in total control over the witness. He either knows what she is going to say or what she has to say based on the evidence or the Rule of Probability.

Mr. Trotter wisely chooses not to cross-examine the witness for the simple reason that he has nothing good to say. Knowing when to speak and when not to are important lessons. Mr. Trotter has now seen his last ditch effort to salvage the case collapse with the indisputable evidence that the defendants' car could not have been the one peeling away from the store. Standing up to "give 'em the ole razzle dazzle" would only discredit himself and his client.

George Wilbur

The defense's second witness was FBI Agent George Wilbur, who is now being recalled as a witness for the defense even though he previously testified for the prosecution.

> Q: In that case, your Honor, I'd like to recall George Wilbur.

J: Miss Vito, you may stand down. [To Wilbur] You realize you're still under oath?

A: Yes, sir.

Q: Mr. Wilbur, how'd you like Miss Vito's testimony?

A: Very impressive.

Q: She's cute too, huh?

A: Very.

J: Mr. Gambini?

Q: Sorry, sorry, your Honor. Mr. Wilbur, in your expert opinion, would you say that everything that Miss Vito said on the stand was 100 percent accurate?

A: I'd have to say that.

Q: And is there any way in the world that the vehicle the defendants were driving made those tire tracks? It's okay, go ahead and say it; they know.

A: Actually, no.

Q: Thank you, no more questions.

Mr. Gambini recalls Mr. Wilbur to extinguish any doubt (to the extent that there could have been after Miss Vito's testimony) that the defendant's car couldn't have been the one that made the tire tracks in question. The witness agrees, of course, because he has no other choice. Another nail in the prosecution's coffin, and Mr. Trotter wisely says nothing.

Sheriff Farley

The final witness for the defense and the last in the case is the Sheriff of Beacham County where the crime took place and where the defendants were arrested.

Q: Sheriff Farley, what'd you find out?

A: On a hunch, I took it upon myself to check out if there was any information on a 1963 Pontiac Tempest, stolen or abandoned recently. This computer readout confirms that two boys, who fit the defendants' description, were arrested two days ago by Sheriff Tillman in Jasper County, Georgia, for driving a stolen metallic mint green 1963 Pontiac Tempest, with a white convertible top, Michelin model XGV tires, size 75 R 14.

Q: Is that it?

A: No. A 357 Magnum revolver was found in their possession.

Q: Sheriff Farley, just to refresh the court's memory, what caliber weapon was used to murder Jimmy Willis?

A: 357 Magnum.

Q: The defense rests.

Q: [Trotter]Your Honor, in light of Miss Vito's and Mr. Wilbur's testimony, the State would like to dismiss all charges.

The final nail in the coffin. We should all be so lucky to have our cases end in such neat bows where the outcome is so clear that, by the end, the other side collapses under the insurmountable weight of the evidence. But that only happens in the movies, like this one.

Sheriff Farley (The Missing Cross-Examination)

A quick note regarding Sheriff Farley. It was never been explained (to my knowledge) why Sheriff Farley was not called by the prosecution to testify given his Preliminary Hearing testimony about the defendant Gambini's confession to shooting the clerk, since Mr. Trotter relied upon that confession in his opening statement.[†]

For our purposes, however, let's assume that Sheriff Farley was called by the prosecution and that he testified on direct examination the same way he did at the Preliminary Hearing about his questioning of the defendant Gambini: "I asked him if he did it and he said 'I shot the clerk.' I asked him again and again he said 'I shot the clerk.'"

How would a cross-examiner deal with such a significant problem as a confession? The first step would be understanding what kind of cross-examination this is and what tools we have to deal with it. Given that this witness claims that the defendant confessed to committing the crime, this is a Credibility Attack cross-examination since the case is over if he is believed. Does the witness have to be a liar or could he have made a mistake? That depends on what tools are available. What tools are available? The

---

† By way of reminder, the relevant portion of Mr. Trotter's opening statement is re-produced here: "Finally, the State is going to prove that the defendants, Gambini and Rothenstein, admitted and then recanted their testimony to the Sheriff of Beacham County."

Indeed, Mr. Trotter also claimed that Mr. Rothenstein had previously confessed to Sheriff Farley. We cannot fully examine this issue since Sheriff Farley did not apparently testify about Mr. Rothstein's confession during the Preliminary Hearing and there was no evidence of it at trial. While this work is not about the strategy of opening statements, suffice it to say that you should not reference evidence during an opening statement unless you intend to actually use it.

only thing available is what was said during the relevant part of the interview, which is re-produced below:‡

Q: When'd you shoot him?
A: What?
Q: At what point did you shoot the clerk?
A: I shot the clerk?
Q: Yes, when did you shoot him?
A: I shot the clerk?

Now the main difference between what was said during the interview and Sheriff Farley's Preliminary Hearing testimony is whether the defendant's last two answers were questions or whether they were statements (i.e., whether there should be question marks or periods at the end of the sentence).

But there are two additional issues with Sheriff Farley's testimony: the interview questions are substantively different and he asked three questions instead of two. So how do we use this to disprove a confession? Let's take a hypothetical look at what the cross-examination could be assuming that the witness is bound to the interview statements, but can disagree about the vocal inflection:

Q: *Sheriff, you claim that Mr. Gambini confessed to shooting the clerk?*
A: *Yes.*

---

‡ Since we may not have Sheriff Farley's entire Preliminary Hearing testimony, we are only using the overlapping portions of Sheriff Farley's testimony and the defendant Gambini's interview for this exercise.

Q: *You testified on direct examination that you asked him two times if he shot the clerk?*

A: *Yes.*

Q: *But you actually asked him three questions instead of two, didn't you?*

A: *Yes.*

Q: *And you didn't actually ask him "if" he shot the clerk those three times, but instead asked him three times "when" he shot the clerk?*

A: *That's right.*

Q: *The first time you asked him when, he said "what?" with a question mark at the end, didn't he?*

A: *That sounds right.*

Q: *And when he said "what?" in response to your question of when he shot the clerk, Mr. Gambini was demonstrating that he didn't know anything about the clerk being shot?*

A: *Well, I thought he may have not have heard the question, which is why I asked him again.*

Q: *After he replied "what?" you then asked him, "at what point did you shoot the clerk?" and he responded with another question, "I shot the clerk?" didn't he?*

A: *I don't agree that he was responding with a question, it was a statement and it was a confession to the crime.*

Q: *You didn't ask Mr. Gambini if he shot the clerk, did you?*

A: *No, I asked him when did he shoot the clerk.*

Q: *You have previously testified under oath that you twice asked him if he shot the clerk?*

A: Yes. I was mistaken about the exact form of the question that I asked. Mr. Gambini nevertheless confessed to shooting Jimmy Willis.

Q: And you were wrong about what the question actually was both times you testified under oath?

A: Yes.

Q: The actual question you asked is very important because Mr. Gambini didn't actually answer the question that you asked him, did he?

A: I don't understand what you mean.

Q: You asked him a second time when did he shoot the clerk and Mr. Gambini didn't tell you when he shot the clerk, did he?

A: No, he didn't.

Q: You asked him when he shot the clerk and he said, "I shot the clerk?" because he didn't know what you were talking about and your question didn't ask him if he shot someone, but instead assumed he had?

A: I don't agree. He confessed to the crime.

Q: You claim that this was a confession, but you didn't stop asking questions about when he shot the clerk, did you?

A: No, I didn't. I wanted to know when he shot him, and he still didn't answer me.

Q: Then in response to his question challenging the assertion you were making, you again asked him when he shot the clerk, didn't you?

A: I did ask him again because I wanted him to answer the question.

Q: *Upon being asked for a third time when he shot the clerk, Mr. Gambini again challenged your assertion the exact same way he did before and said, "I shot the clerk?"*

A: *He didn't ask a question. This was a confession.*

Q: *So, you asked him three times when he shot the clerk and his three answers never answered your questions, did they?*

A: *Not directly, no.*

Q: *You asked him three times when he shot the clerk and his three answers were "what?" "I shot the clerk?" and "I shot the clerk?"*

A: *That's the substance of what he said, but I disagree with how you are characterizing his vocal inflection. He last two answers were not questions, he confessed.*

Q: *Your disagreement with the nature of his vocal inflection is based on your memory?*

A: *Yes.*

Q: *And when you twice testified falsely about the actual questions you asked during the interview, this was also based on your memory, wasn't it?*

A: *It was. I made a mistake those times, but I am not making one now.*

While no one can say how a trier of fact would decide the outcome of this issue, I am confident that this is the best way to attack the credibility of the witness's version of events and present an alternative argument given the tools available. In this "he said, he said" battle about whether the defendant's answers were statements or questions, the best tools we have are the witness's inaccurate testimony about how many questions were asked and the substance of the questions.

To the extent we can cast doubt on things he got wrong, it is more likely that he got other things wrong as well. Indeed, the missing question and answer, as well as the difference between asking "when" instead of "if" the defendant shot the clerk dramatically increases the persuasiveness of the argument that the defendant's answers were not a confession. The key was identifying the available tools by reviewing the witness's previous statements, using the power of organization to make the argument more persuasive, and relying upon the Rule of Probability to win the credibility contest about which version of events was more likely.

Summary

My Cousin Vinny is a favorite of trial lawyers since it is one of the best trial movies.[§] If you have previously seen it, I am confident that you now see it differently through the lens of our strategy and techniques.

The clean Hollywood ending does not matter, but what does is seeing how the cross-examiner used the techniques to argue the case through the witness. Mr. Gambini ably demonstrated that we do not have to robotically use leading questions, demand only yes or no answers, or show

---

§ Indeed, *My Cousin Vinny* is frequently referenced by lawyers and even cited by judges, given its rich legal issues. Some examples are a 2019 Opinion by Merrick Garland, then Chief Judge of the District of Columbia Court of Appeals, and a 2006 Opinion by Antonin Scalia, then an Associate Justice of the United States Supreme Court.

that all of the other side's witness are liars. As we saw with Mr. Gibbons's excellent demonstration of what *not* to do, a cross-examination is only successful if our boat is aimed in the right strategic direction and if we correctly utilize the techniques to get us there.

CHAPTER NINETEEN

United States vs. Lance Corporal Harold W. Dawson and Private First Class Loudon Downey

H ere is our second case study. We will also go through this trial to analyze the strategy and techniques that the cross-examiners use. As we shall see, the issues will sometimes appear similar to our first case study, and sometimes they will be different. That is hardly surprising. The cases are different, and the issues they present will therefore vary. It is that uniqueness that makes trial advocacy such an interesting and rewarding discipline. Nonetheless, the techniques available to the cross-examiner—the tools of the trade—are constant from case to case.

Here is the background of the case. In 1989, Lance Corporal Harold W. Dawson and Private First Class Loudon Downey were marines assigned to the Guantanamo Bay Naval Base in Cuba. One evening, Corporal Dawson and Private Downey entered the room of a fellow marine, Private First Class William T. Santiago. They then shoved a rag in Private Santiago's mouth before he could scream, placed duct tape over the rag in his mouth, bound his wrists behind his back, and then bound his ankles together with the duct tape. Private Santiago subsequently died at the base hospital approximately one hour later. None of this is in dispute.

Corporal Dawson and Private Downey were charged in a General Court-Martial with Conspiracy to Commit Murder, Murder in the First Degree, and Conduct Unbecoming a United States Marine. The prosecution's theory of the case is that Corporal Dawson and Private Downey murdered Private Santiago by poisoning the rag that they shoved into his throat and sealed in with the duct tape. The prosecution claimed they did this because Private Santiago had written letters to outside investigators offering, in exchange for a transfer off of the base, to provide information that Corporal Dawson had illegally discharged his weapon over the fence line from United States soil into Cuban territory.

The defendants deny having any intent to kill Private Santiago, maintain that the rag was not poisoned, and claim that they were only following the orders of a superior officer to give Private Santiago a "Code Red" (a form of inter-squad punishment) for Private Santiago's having gone outside the chain of command in reporting the allegations against Corporal Dawson.

Opening Statements

Captain Jack Ross gave the following opening statement on behalf of the United States:

> The facts of the case are this: At midnight on September 6, the defendants went into the barracks

room of their platoon-mate, PFC William Santiago. They woke him up, tied his arms and legs with tape, and forced a rag into his throat. A few minutes later, a chemical reaction in Santiago's body called lactic acidosis caused his lungs to begin bleeding. He drowned in his own blood and was pronounced dead at thirty-seven minutes past midnight. These are the facts of the case. And they are undisputed. That's right. The story I just told you is the exact same story you're going to hear from Corporal Dawson, and it's the exact same story you're going to hear from Private Downey. Furthermore, the government will also demonstrate that the defendants soaked the rag with poison, and entered Santiago's room with motive and intent to kill. Now, Lt. Kaffee is gonna try to pull off a little magic act, he's gonna try a little misdirection. He's going to astonish you with stories of rituals and dazzle you with official sounding terms like Code Red. He might even cut into a few officers for you. He'll have no evidence, mind you, none. But it's gonna be entertaining. When we get to the end, all the magic in the world will not have been able to divert your attention from the fact that Willy Santiago is dead, and Dawson and Downey killed him. These are the facts of the case. And they are undisputed.[6]

Lieutenant Daniel Kaffee then made an opening statement on behalf of Lance Corporal Harold W. Dawson and Private First Class Loudon Downey:

There was no poison on the rag and there was no intent to kill and any attempt to prove otherwise is futile because it just ain't true. When Dawson and Downey went into Santiago's room that night, it wasn't because of vengeance or hatred; it wasn't to kill or harm; and it wasn't because they were looking for kicks on a Friday night. It's because it was what they were ordered to do. Let me say that again: It's because it was what they were ordered to do. Now, out in the real world, that means nothing. And here at the Washington Navy Yard, it doesn't mean a whole lot more. But if you're a marine assigned to Rifle Security Company Windward, Guantanamo Bay, Cuba, and you're given an order, you follow it or you pack your bags. Make no mistake about it; Harold Dawson and Louden Downey are sitting before you in judgment today because they did their job.

Robert C. McGuire

The prosecution's first witness was Robert C. McGuire, who testified on direct examination:

Q: Mr. McGuire, would you state your full name and occupation for the record, please?
A: Robert C. McGuire, Special Agent, Naval Investigative Service.
Q: Mr. McGuire, did your office receive a letter from PFC William Santiago on 3 September of this year?
A: We did.
Q: What did the letter say?

A: That a member of Private Santiago's unit had illegally fired his weapon over the fence line.

Q: Was that marine identified in the letter?

A: No sir. I notified the barracks CO, Colonel Jessep, that I would be coming down to investigate.

Q: And what did you find?

A: For the shift reported, only one sentry returned his weapon to the switch with a round of ammunition missing.

Q: And who was that?

A: Lance Corporal Harold Dawson.

Q: Your witness.

The prosecution's first witness is presented to establish the motive for why the defendants killed Private Santiago: to stop him from making the illegal discharge allegation against Corporal Dawson. Lt. Kaffee then cross-examines on behalf of the defendants:

Q: Mr. McGuire, have you questioned Corporal Dawson about the fence line shooting?

A: Yes. He claims to have been engaged in some manner by the enemy.

For his first question in the case, Lt. Kaffee chooses to use a controlled open-ended question to establish that Corporal Dawson maintained his innocence regarding the fence line shooting allegation. It is a fine place to begin since Lt. Kaffee knows that Corporal Dawson denied the allegations to the investigator, so no answer can hurt him and the full answer is more persuasive coming from the witness rather than a simple yes or no.

Q: But you don't believe him.
A: It's not my place—

Lt. Kaffee's second question, however, is a mistake because it has no viable strategic purpose. Like Mr. Gibbons from our previous case study, this second question indicates that this entire cross-examination is headed for trouble because no answer the witness can give is good for the defense. Lt. Kaffee has followed Sammy's Rule and became willfully blind to his ability to counter the direct examination.

Pursuant to the evidence and the Rule of Probability, this witness is not going to say that he believes Corporal Downey, so the only other options are for the witness to say he does not believe Corporal Downey or that he doesn't have enough information to know. Either answer is bad for the defense since it all leads to the same place in the end. We can clearly see that a good or bad cross-examination question does not depend simply on whether it is open or closed, but whether it has information that can control the witness to advance the theory of the case.

Q: Corporal Dawson's been charged with a number of crimes, why wasn't he charged with firing at the enemy without cause?
A: There wasn't enough evidence to support such a charge.
Q: Thank you.

This is the same kind of pretend victory that we previously saw in Mr. Gibbons's cross-examination of Sam
Tipton over his eye glasses. Lt. Kaffee thinks he has bolstered his case by demonstrating that Corporal Dawson
was not guilty of the fence line shooting allegation and
therefore did not have motive to kill Private Santiago.
Perhaps this type of strategy could be successful in a system where no one else is allowed to ask questions of a witness, but the prosecutor is about to show us how things
work in the adversarial system. He uses the blundering
cross—which suggested that Corporal Dawson was not
charged because he did not fire his weapon—to bolster
his argument that the accused had a motive to murder the
only witness.

Captain Ross on re-direct:

Q: Mr. McGuire, I don't understand what you mean
when you say there wasn't enough evidence to sup-
port such a charge. You had Willy Santiago's letter.
A: Santiago was the only witness, but I never had a
chance to interview him. So I don't know what he
saw.
Q: And now we won't ever know, will we, Mr.
McGuire?
A: No.
Q: No more questions.

It is painful indeed when your cross-examination ends up
bolstering your adversary's motive theory. The fatal flaw of
Lt. Kaffee's cross-examination strategy was his goal of demonstrating that Corporal Dawson did not have motive to kill

Private Santiago because he was innocent or there wasn't enough evidence to charge him in the fence line shooting.

Based on the facts of the case, that was simply not attainable and pursuing it has damaged Lt. Kaffee's credibility. There can be no sensible dispute that Private Santiago was offering incriminating evidence against Corporal Dawson and that Private Santiago died before he could be questioned about it. As such, this strategy is a bridge too far. To add insult to injury, it was Lt. Kaffee's cross-examination that gave rise to the line of questioning on re-direct that Private Santiago died before he could be interviewed, which the prosecution failed to develop during the direct examination.

In the end, Lt. Kaffee asked three cross-examination questions and the last two served to bolster the prosecution's case against his clients while diminishing his own credibility. The only positive information he elicited was that Corporal Dawson denied the fence line shooting allegations when questioned. As such, Lt. Kaffee should have, at most, asked the first question and ended it there with a limited Hitchhiking strategy.

Corporal Carl Edward Hammaker

The prosecution's second witness was Corporal Carl Edward Hammaker, who testified on direct examination:

> Q: Corporal, were you present at a meeting that Lt. Kendrick held on the afternoon of September 6 with the members of second platoon?
>
> A: Yes, sir.

Q: Would you tell the Court the substance of that meeting?

A: Lt. Kendrick told us that we had an informer in our group. That Private Santiago had gone outside the chain of command and reported to the NIS on a member of our platoon.

Q: Did that make you mad? You can tell the truth, corporal, it's alright. Did it make you mad?

A: Yes, sir.

Q: How mad?

A: Private Santiago betrayed a code that we believe in very deeply, sir.

Q: Were the other members of the squad angry?

Q: [Kaffee] Objection.

Q: Were Dawson and Downey?

Q: [Kaffee] Please the Court, is the judge advocate honestly asking this witness to testify as to how the defendant felt on September 6?

J: Sustained.

Q: Corporal, did Lt. Kendrick leave a standing order at that meeting?

A: Yes, sir.

Q: What was it?

A: Well, it was clear that he didn't want us to take matters into our own hands, sir.

Q: What was the order?

A: Sir, he said that Santiago wasn't to be touched.

Q: Your witness.

The prosecution's second witness is presented to establish that 1) the defendants knew that Private Santiago had informed on Corporal Dawson, which bolsters the motive argument; and 2) that not only were the defendants not ordered to give Private Santiago a "Code Red" as they claim, but were publicly and specifically instructed along with the other members of the platoon not to touch Private Santiago.

Lt. Kaffee then cross-examines on behalf of the defendants:

> Q: Corporal Hammaker, were you in Dawson and Downey's barracks room ten minutes after this meeting?
>
> A: No, sir.
>
> Q: Thanks, I have no more questions.

Lt. Kaffee uses a single controlled opened ended question utilizing the Limiting technique to demonstrate the witness's lack of knowledge. Lt. Kaffee, however, does not make full use of what is available.

First, his question is too opaque to pack the necessary punch with the trier of fact. Remember, Lt. Kaffee has already said in his opening statement that the defendants were ordered to do this to Private Santiago. As such, there is no reason to exclude this from his question. Indeed, Lt. Kaffee's question should make clear what the witness does not have knowledge of (i.e., that Lt. Kendrick went to their barracks room ten minutes after the meeting and gave a contrary order for a Code Red to be given to Private Santiago). For example:

> Q: *Corporal Hammaker, you are not in a position to know whether or not Lt. Kendrick ordered a Code*

> *Red on Private Santiago in Dawson and Downey's*
> *room ten minutes after the meeting?*

The witness's answer would of course be the same, but stating your theory of defense through the form of the question is more persuasive to the trier of fact. Second, Lt. Kaffee missed another area to limit this witness's knowledge and to provide potentially helpful information. The witness only testified that:

> **A:** Lt. Kendrick told us that we had an informer in our group. That Private Santiago had gone outside the chain of command and reported to the NIS on a *member* of our platoon. [Emphasis added.]

As such, this testimony indicates that Corporal Dawson's name was never mentioned nor was the particular situation that Private Santiago was informing about described with particularity. The fact that these details were not communicated to the squad during the meeting is helpful to the defense because it potentially negates their motive.

While the outcome of this witness was not as bad as the first one, Lt. Kaffee has nevertheless missed important opportunities to advance his theory of the case through a more robust utilization of the Limiting technique and the failure to identify the Hitchhiking opportunity.

Commander Dr. Walter Stone

The prosecution's third witness was Commander Dr. Walter Stone, who testified on direct examination in relevant part:

Q: Dr. Stone, what's lactic acidosis?

A: If the muscles and other cells of the body burn sugar instead of oxygen, lactic acid is produced. That lactic acid is what caused Santiago's lungs to bleed.

Q: How long does it take for the muscles and other cells to begin burning sugar instead of oxygen?

A: Twenty to thirty minutes.

Q: And what caused Santiago's muscles and other cells to start burning sugar?

A: An ingested poison of some kind.

Q: [Kaffee] Your Honor, we object at this point. The witness is speculating.

Q: Commander Stone is an expert medical witness; in this courtroom his opinion isn't considered speculation.

Q: [Kaffee] Commander Stone is an internist, not a criminologist, and the medical facts here are ultimately inconclusive.

J: A point which I'm confident you'll illustrate to the jury under cross-examination, so I'm sure you won't mind if his opinion is admitted now.

Q: [Kaffee] Not at all, sir. Objection withdrawn.

Notice how Lt. Kaffee handles losing this objection. It was certainly an objection worth making (assuming it couldn't be done pre-trial) since the question of whether there was or was not poison should determine the outcome of the case. Simply put, if there was poison on the rag, the defendants will be convicted of murder since it would be irrefutable evidence of their intent to kill Private Santiago and would destroy the defense's argument that his death was accidental.

Lt. Kaffee has lost the objection, but the judge has made it clear that the issue of whether or not poison was present is still an open issue for cross-examination. Moreover, the judge understands the importance of an advocate's credibility and gives Lt. Kaffee the opportunity to withdraw the objection with grace. Make no mistake, the judge has ruled against him, but has offered a face saving "I'm sure you won't mind" rather than an "Overruled." Understanding this, Lt. Kaffee wisely accepts the offer.

Q: Doctor Stone, did Willy Santiago die of poisoning?
A: Absolutely.
Q: Are you aware that the lab report and the coroner's report showed no traces of poison?
A: Yes, I am.
Q: Then how do you justify—
A: There are literally dozens of toxins which are virtually undetectable, both in the human body and on a fabric. The nature of the acidosis is the compelling factor in this issue.
Q: Thank you, sir.

There is no more critical issue in this case than whether or not the defendants placed poison on the rag since it would serve as concrete evidence of their intent to murder Private Santiago and directly refute their defense that they were just following orders to give him a non-lethal "Code Red." Dr. Stone has taken the position that Private

Santiago "absolutely" died from poison, and the defense must refute this conclusion.

Lt. Kaffee cross-examines on behalf of the defendants:

> Q: Commander, you testified that it takes lactic acidosis twenty to thirty minutes before it becomes lethal.
>
> A: Yes.
>
> Q: Let me ask you: is it possible for a person to have an affliction, some sort of condition, which might, in the case of this person, actually speed up the process of acidosis dramatically?
>
> A: Certainly.

Lt. Kaffee's controlled open-ended question begins the unfurling of the defense's theory about how Private Santiago died: that he had an underlying condition that caused his lungs to bleed when the rag was put into his throat.

> Q: What might some of those conditions be?
>
> A: If a person had a coronary disorder . . . or a cerebral disorder, the process would be more rapid.

Lt. Kaffee uses another controlled open-ended question to force the doctor into saying what the conditions were. Lt. Kaffee already knows the conditions, but having the doctor say them instead of a simple "yes" or "no" is more persuasive since it appears that the witness is not being controlled.

> Q: Commander, if I had a coronary condition, and a perfectly clean rag was placed in my mouth, and

the rag was accidentally pushed too far down, is
it possible that my cells would continue burning
sugar after the rag was taken out?

A: It would have to be a very serious condition.

Lt. Kaffee has used a "hypothetical," which is of course
actually his theory of defense, to get the doctor to go a
step further than before: that someone with a coronary
condition could continue suffering from lactic acidosis
even after a poison-free rag was removed.

The beauty of this question is that Lt. Kaffee is able
to put forward two of the essential defenses, that "the rag
was accidentally pushed too far down" and that the defendants removed the rag when they saw Private Santiago
bleeding, which would negate their intent to commit
first degree murder. The witness is forced to concede,
but seeks to protect his position by moving the goalposts
in an attempt to head this off before it puts him into a
tighter box.

Q: Is it possible to have a serious coronary condition,
where the initial warning signals were so mild as to
escape a physician during a routine medical exam?

A: Possibly. There would still be symptoms though.

Lt. Kaffee again uses a controlled open-ended question to
elicit an important building block to the argument that
Private Santiago died from an underlying coronary condition, and that such a serious condition could nevertheless
be present without detection in a marine who undergoes
physical examinations. Notice the witness has volunteered

an answer beyond the scope of the question, and Lt. Kaffee wisely seizes on it.

> Q: What kind of symptoms?
> A: There are hundreds of symptoms of a—
> Q: Chest pains?
> A: Yes.
> Q: Shortness of breath?
> A: Yes.
> Q: Fatigue?
> A: Of course.

Lt. Kaffee starts with a controlled open-ended question, but cuts the witness off. It is generally ill-advised to cut off a witness's answer, especially when the answer is not problematic. The witness seemed to be answering that there are hundreds of symptoms a person could have in conjunction with an undetected serious coronary condition. Far from causing harm, more symptoms only helps support the defense's case theory. And who knows what good things the witness may have delivered in this stressed position before he was cut off? But Lt. Kaffee redeems himself by drawing out each symptom in detail and uses each of those details to hammer the witness and thereby the prosecution's case.

> Q: Doctor, is this your signature?
> A: Yes, it is.
> Q: This in an order for Private Santiago to be put on restricted duty. Would you read your handwritten remarks at the bottom of the page, please, sir?

A: "Initial testing negative. Patient complains of chest pains, shortness of breath, and fatigue. Restricted from running distances over five miles for one week."

Excellent. Lt. Kaffee has forced the witness to read his own words rather than asking if the witness wrote them. The result is that the witness's own examination notes confirm that Private Santiago suffered from the same conditions that the witness just said would be symptoms of an undiagnosed and serious coronary condition. Rather than simply asking the witness "yes" or "no" questions, Lt. Kaffee was far more persuasive to the trier of fact by making the witness impeach himself.

Q: Commander, isn't it possible that Santiago had a serious coronary condition, and it was that condition, and not some mysterious poison, that caused the accelerated chemical reaction?

A: No. I personally give the men a physical examination every three months. And every three months Private Santiago got a clean bill of health.

Now it gets very interesting. Some would argue that Lt. Kaffee shouldn't ask this controlled open-ended question because the witness will never agree with him, and that this is a classic example of one question too far because the jury will have almost certainly come to the conclusion by themselves.

I do not share this view. This witness is going to find a way to say these things, whether on cross-examination or on re-direct, because he is in trouble and needs to help himself. Thus, my view is that it is better to deal with it rather than close our eyes to it and hope it goes away (Sammy's Rule).

> Q: And that's why it had to be, poison, right, Commander? Cause Lord knows, if you put a man with a serious coronary condition back on duty with a clean bill of health, and that man died from a heart-related incident, you'd have a lot to answer for, wouldn't you, doctor?
>
> Q: [Ross] Object. Move to strike.
>
> J: Sustained. Strike it.
>
> Q: No more questions, Judge.

This last question is an unfortunate end to an excellent cross-examination. Not only is it a substantively bad question and a poor strategic choice to accuse the witness of being a liar, but Lt. Kaffee suffers the indignity of the judge reprimanding him in front of the jury.

Lt. Kaffee was, however, doing well until this point and even had a better argument to make. Let's clearly understand what other choices he had and why he ended incorrectly. There are two pieces of information that Lt. Kaffee should have used in his cross-examination.

First, Lt. Kaffee previously elicited a very important concession from the witness, who agreed that it was "possible for someone to have a serious coronary condition, where the initial warning signals were so mild as to escape a physician during a routine medical exam." This fact should have then been used as the tool to deal with the witness's subsequent pushback that there must have been poison since he personally gave Private Santiago a physical every three months and always received a clean bill of health.

Second, Lt. Kaffee objected during the witness's direct examination about his ability to render an expert opinion since "Commander Stone is an internist, not a criminologist, and the medical facts here are ultimately inconclusive." The judge overruled the objection, but pointed out that this would be a fertile area for cross-examination, "[a] point which I'm confident you'll illustrate to the jury under cross-examination, so I'm sure you won't mind if his opinion is admitted now." Lt. Kaffee nevertheless failed to make his own argument on cross-examination even after being encouraged to do so by the judge. We will examine how this could have been done after seeing Captain Ross's re-direct:

Q: Dr. Stone, you've held a license to practice medicine for twenty-one years, you are board certified in internal medicine, you are the chief of internal medicine at a hospital, which serves over eight thousand men. In your professional opinion, was Willy Santiago poisoned?

Q: [Downey's Counsel] Your Honor, we renew our objection to Commander Stone's testimony, and ask that it be stricken from the record. And we further ask that the Court instruct the jury to lend no weight to this witness's testimony.

J: The objection's overruled, counsel.

Q: [Downey's Counsel] Sir, the defense strenuously objects and requests a meeting in chambers so that

his honor might have an opportunity to hear dis-
cussion before ruling on the objection.

J: The objection of the defense has been heard and
overruled.

Q: [Downey's Counsel] Exception.

J: Noted. The witness is an expert and the court will
hear his opinion.

Q: Doctor, in your expert, professional opinion, was
Willy Santiago poisoned?

A: Yes.

Q: Thank you, sir, I have no more questions.

That turned into a nightmare pretty quickly. Seizing
upon Lt. Kaffee's inability to make the necessary cross-
examination points and then being chastised by the
judge for his last question, Captain Ross goes for the
jugular by burnishing the witness's credentials and having the witness repeat that the defendants poisoned
Private Santiago.

And if that weren't bad enough, Lt. Kaffee's co-counsel makes matters even worse by: 1) re-making the same
objection the defense already lost; 2) making the same
objection for a third time after being overruled again; 3)
and then still continuing to speak on the issue. None of this
was going stop the witness from saying again that Private
Santiago was poisoned. The only thing that Lt. Kaffee's
co-counsel accomplished was buttressing the prosecution's
case and damaging the defense's credibility.

But do recall, this train wreck traces back to Lt.
Kaffee's last cross-examination question. I would propose
that Lt. Kaffee's cross-examination should have ended

with something like this, with the answers that any rational person would be forced to make (and the answers that everyone would hear nevertheless):

Q: *Dr. Stone, you just claimed that it was impossible for Private Santiago to have had a serious coronary condition since you personally examined him every three months and that every three months you gave him a clean bill of health?*

A: *Yes.*

Q: *Do you recall that I previously asked you the following question, "Is it possible to have a serious coronary condition, where the initial warning signals were so mild as to escape a physician during a routine medical exam?" and you answered, "Possibly. There would still be symptoms though"?*

A: *Yes.*

Q: *Given your testimony that it is possible for a serious coronary condition's initial warning signals to be so mild that it could escape a physician during a routine medical exam, it was certainly possible for such a condition to be undiscovered when you performed routine medical exams on Private Santiago?*

A: *Yes.*

Q: *Not only is it possible that Private Santiago's serious coronary condition could have escaped detection during your physical of him, but he complained of chest pains, shortness of breath, and fatigue, didn't he?*

A: *He did.*

Q: *And in response to those symptoms, you put Private Santiago on restricted duty, keeping him from running distances over five miles for one week?*

A: *Yes.*

Q: *Now Dr. Stone, both the lab report and the coroner's report showed no traces of poison?*

A: *That's true, but as I previously testified, there are literally dozens of toxins that are virtually undetectable, both in the human body and on a fabric. The nature of the acidosis is the compelling factor in this issue.*

Q: *Dr. Stone, you are not a criminologist, are you?*

A: *Correct, I am an internist.*

Q: *Notwithstanding the fact that you are an internist with no experience in criminology, you are nevertheless 100 percent certain that the cause of death was from poison, even though no poison was detected and the lactic acidosis could have been caused by a serious coronary condition consistent with the symptoms that Private Santiago was suffering from?*

A: *Yes, he was poisoned.*

Now you may be saying, "but you didn't get the witness to change his testimony?" That's true. But the jury was answering the last question even as the witness did. And it is inconceivable that their answers agreed with the witness's. In one sense, the witness's answers became irrelevant. But in the largest sense, his last answer destroyed the prosecution's theory that it was intended to help because it became not credible.

Corporal Jeffrey Owen Howard

After Dr. Stone's testimony, the prosecution rested its case, confident that its three witnesses established that the defendants had a motive to kill Private Santiago, were specifically ordered not to touch him by a commanding officer, and that they used poison to kill him, per an expert opinion. Even though the outcome of the case does not matter for our purposes, it is relevant insofar as it indicates how the cross-examinations went. On that score, it is fair to say that the defense's cross-examinations went very poorly given what could have been accomplished.

The defense's first witness was Corporal Jeffrey Owen Howard, who testified on direct examination:

> Q: Corporal Howard, name some reasons why a marine would get a Code Red?
> A: Being late for platoon or company meetings, keeping his barracks in disorder, falling back on a run
> . . .
> Q: Have you ever received a Code Red?
> A: Yes, sir. We were doing seven man assault drills, and my weapon slipped. It's just cause it was over a hundred degrees and my palms were sweaty and I'd forgot to use the resin like we were taught.
> Q: And what happened?
> A: That night the guys in my squad threw a blanket over me and took turns punching me in the arm for five minutes. Then they poured glue on my hands.

And it worked, too, cause I ain't never dropped my weapon since.

Q: Was Private Santiago ever late for platoon meetings?

A: Yes, sir.

Q: Was his barracks ever in disorder?

A: Yes, sir.

Q: Did he ever fall back on a run?

A: All the time, sir.

Q: Did he ever, prior to the night of September 6, receive a Code Red?

A: No, sir.

Q: Never?

A: No, sir.

Q: You got a code red cause your palms were sweaty. Why didn't Santiago, this burden to his unit, ever get one?

A: Dawson wouldn't allow it, sir.

Q: Dawson wouldn't allow it?

A: The guys talked tough about Santiago, but they wouldn't go near him. They were too afraid of Dawson, sir.

Q: [Ross] Object. The witness is characterizing.

Q: I'll rephrase. Jeffrey, did you ever want to give Santiago a Code Red?

A: Yes, sir.

Q: Why didn't you?

A: Cause Dawson'd kick my butt, sir.

Q: Good enough. Lt. Ross is gonna ask you some questions now.

The defense is trying to establish two things with this witness: 1) that Code Reds existed on the base as well as the nature of them and; 2) that Corporal Dawson had been a protector of Private Santiago. On the first point, the defense is successful in establishing the existence of a Code Red, but fails to go far enough in establishing whether commanding officers issued Code Reds and if someone could have refused such an order.

The second point, that Corporal Dawson protected Private Santiago, is negated by the fact that Corporal Dawson's defense is that he gave Private Santiago a Code Red. The explanation that the defense could have potentially made is that Corporal Dawson would not have harmed Private Santiago or given him a Code Red unless he was ordered to since he previously stopped non-superior officers from doing it.

Captain Ross cross-examines for the prosecution:

Q: Corporal Howard, I hold here *The Marine Guide and General Information Handbook for New Recruits.* Are you familiar with this book?

A: Yes, sir.

Q: Have you read it?

A: Yes, sir.

Q: Good. Would you turn to the chapter that deals with Code Reds, please?

A: Sir?

Q: Just flip to the page in that book that discusses Code Reds.

A: Sir, you see, Code Red is a term we use—it's just used down at GITMO, sir. I don't know if it actually—

Q: We're in luck, then. *The Marine Corps Guide for
Sentry Duty, NAVY BASE Guantanamo Bay,
Cuba.* I assume we'll find the term code red and its
definition in this book, am I correct?

A: No, sir.

Q: No? Corporal Howard, I'm a marine. Is there no
book, no manual or pamphlet, no set of orders or
regulations that let me know that, as a marine, one
of my duties is to perform Code Reds?

A: No, sir. No books, sir.

Q: No further questions.

Captain Ross does a fine job of using controlled open-
ended questions to make his point that Code Reds are not
codified in any manual. But that does little for the prosecution's ability to prove its case since the witness claims
Code Reds exist, and there is no challenge to that. The
point that they are not written down in any manual does
not support the prosecution's theory that this was not a
Code Red, given this witness's testimony that they do exist.

Like many of the lawyers we have analyzed thus far,
Captain Ross's form of the question is not the problem. It
is his strategy for dealing with this witness. Captain Ross
must accept that Code Reds are real and occur on the base,
because there is evidence to support it and he doesn't have
evidence to disprove it. We will look at how this could
have been done better after seeing Lt. Kaffee's re-direct.

Lt. Kaffee re-directs for the defense:

Q: Corporal, would you turn to the page in this book
that says where the enlisted men's mess hall is?

A: Lt. Kaffee, that's not in the book, sir.

Q: I don't understand, how did you know where the enlisted men's mess hall was if it's not in this book?

A: I guess I just followed the crowd at chow time, sir.

Q: No more questions.

Lt. Kaffee seizes on Captain Ross's ill-advised cross-examination theme to knock down the empty argument that Code Reds don't exist on the base because they are not codified.

Instead of pursuing this impossible mission, Captain Ross should have determined what was possible or instead should have said nothing. For me, the persuasive cross-examination is instead whether this was in fact a Code Red or an intentional murder using a poisoned rag in order to keep Private Santiago from destroying Corporal Dawson's career and life. Here is an example of a more effective cross-examination utilizing the Limiting and Hitchhiking techniques:

Q: *Corporal Howard, were you aware that Private Santiago was offering incriminating testimony to investigators against Corporal Dawson for his illegal fence line shooting into Cuban territory in exchange for a transfer off of the base?*

A: *No, I was not.*

Q: *Are you aware that on the same night that Private Santiago was killed by Corporal Dawson and Private Downey, that they both became aware that Private Santiago was offering the incriminating evidence against Corporal Dawson to investigators?*

A: No.

Q: *Corporal Howard, you testified that Corporal Dawson had never allowed anyone to give Private Santiago a Code Red?*

A: Yes.

Q: *After protecting Private Santiago for all of this time, Corporal Dawson now claims that he was giving Private Santiago a Code Red on the same night he found out that Private Santiago was offering incriminating evidence against him. Do you have any evidence that anyone ordered him or Private Downey to give Private Santiago a Code Red?*

A: No, I don't.

Q: *Do you have any evidence that anyone ordered Corporal Dawson and Private Downey to stuff a rag with poison down Private Santiago's throat on the same night they found out that Private Santiago was offering incriminating evidence against Corporal Dawson?*

A: No, I don't.

Q: *Corporal Howard, have you ever heard of a Code Red where someone puts poison on a rag and then shoves that rag down the person's throat after binding their arms and legs?*

A: No, I haven't.

This demonstrative cross-examination is more effective than Captain Ross's since it uses the Limiting and Hitchhiking techniques to show the limits of the witness's knowledge and to co-opt (rather than futilely fight) the witness's testimony about the existence of Code Reds and make the argument that the defendants' conduct doesn't fit the profile of a Code Red.

Second Lieutenant Jonathan Kendrick

The defense's second witness was Second Lt. Jonathan Kendrick. While this is technically a direct examination, the witness is adverse to the defense so we will analyze it as the cross-examination that it was.

> Q: Lt. Kendrick, in your opinion, was Private Santiago a good marine?
> A: I'd say he was about average.
> Q: Lieutenant, you signed three fitness reports on Santiago. On all three reports you indicated a rating of Below Average.
> A: Yes. Private Santiago was Below Average. I didn't see the need in trampling on a man's grave.

An excellent identification of the opportunity to Pull the Chain and then use the witness's prior inconsistent statement as the impeachment tool. This is another example of when witnesses will hurt themselves unnecessarily.

> Q: We appreciate that, but you're under oath now, and I think unpleasant as it may be, we'd all just as soon hear the truth.
> A: I'm aware of my oath.

While Lt. Kaffee did a good job of impeaching the witness with the prior statement, his response is poor. Lt. Kaffee accepts the premise of the witness's reason for the false answer, which gives it credibility. Lt. Kaffee should have instead exposed it and attacked the witness's credibility. For example: "Lieutenant, you were lying when you said that Private Santiago was an average marine, weren't you?" Depending on his answer this could hopefully go on for a while. The more witnesses play games, lie, or obfuscate, it gives more opportunity to damage their credibility.

Lt. Kaffee continued:

Q: Lieutenant, these are the last three fitness reports you signed for Lance Corporal Dawson and PFC Downey. Downey received three straight marks of Exceptional. Dawson received two marks of Exceptional, but on this most recent report, dated June 9 of this year, he received a rating of Below Average. It's this last report that I'd like to discuss for a moment.

A: That's fine.

Q: Lance Corporal Dawson's ranking after Infantry Training School was perfect. Records indicate that over half that class has since been promoted to full corporal, while Dawson has remained a lance corporal. Was Dawson's promotion held up because of this last fitness report?

A: I'm sure it was.

Q: Do you recall why Dawson was given such a poor grade on this report?

A: I'm sure I don't. I have many men in my charge, Lieutenant. I write many fitness reports.

Q: Do you recall an incident involving a PFC Curtis Bell who'd been found stealing liquor from the Officer's Club?

A: Yes.

Q: Did you report Private Bell to the proper authorities?

A: I have two books at my bedside, Lieutenant, the *Marine Code of Conduct* and the King James Bible. The only proper authorities I'm aware of are my commanding officer, Colonel Nathan R. Jessup, and the Lord our God.

Q: Lt. Kendrick, at your request, I can have the record reflect your lack of acknowledgment of this court as a proper authority.

Q: [Ross] Objection. Argumentative.

J: Sustained. Watch yourself, counselor.

Another missed opportunity for Lt. Kaffee to Pull the Chain. Instead of treating this as a gift and making it into a positive, Lt. Kaffee incredibly turned it into a negative where he gets reprimanded by the judge. Here's an example of how this could be done to attack the witness's credibility:

Q: *Lt., you just testified that your only proper authorities are your commanding officer, Col. Nathan R. Jessup, and the Lord our God?*

A: *Yes.*

Q: *Your list of proper authorities did not include this court. Is that why you intentionally lied when I previously asked you whether Private Santiago was a good marine despite your oath to tell the truth?*

> A: *I was only trying to speak well of the dead, and I do respect this court's authority.*

Anytime that this witness gives us the opportunity to bring this up, we should take it. Back to Lt. Kaffee:

> Q: Did you report Private Bell to your superiors?
> A: I remember thinking very highly of Private Bell, and not wanting to see his record tarnished by a formal charge.
> Q: You preferred it to be handled within the unit.
> A: I most certainly did.

More missed opportunities to damage the witness's credibility and advance the defense theory. These answers do not comport with the previous answers and Lt. Kaffee has let him get away with it. Here's an example of how this could be done:

> Q: *Instead of answering my previous question about whether you reported Private Bell, you told us that other than God, the only other proper authority that you acknowledged was your commanding officer, true?*
> A: *Yes.*
> Q: *Did you report him to your commanding officer?*
> A: *No. I remember thinking very highly of Private Bell, and not wanting to see his record tarnished by a formal charge.*
> Q: *So, you didn't even respect your commanding officer as a proper authority when you decided to withhold this information from them?*

A: I preferred to handle it within the unit so that Private Bell's record would not be tarnished.

Q: And instead of doing what you were required to do, you took it upon yourself to mete out an unauthorized punishment to Private Bell without informing your commanding officer?

A: I did.

Notice how the witness's answers throughout this cross-examination have created stress positions for him. The cross-examiner should use the witness's answers to demonstrate that he is not credible and to argue that Private Santiago died as a result of an intra-squad punishment ordered by Lt. Kendrick. Back to Lt. Kaffee:

Q: Lieutenant, do you know what a Code Red is?

A: Yes, I do.

Q: Have you ever ordered a Code Red?

A: No, I have not.

Q: Lieutenant, did you order Dawson and two other men to make sure that Private Bell receive no food or drink except water for a period of seven days?

A: That's a distortion of the truth. Private Bell was placed on barracks restriction. He was given water and vitamin supplements, and I assure you that at no time was his health in danger.

Q: I'm sure it was lovely for Private Bell, but you did order the barracks restriction, didn't you? And you did order the denial of food.

A: Yes.

Lt. Kaffee has made a significant error here. The witness has claimed that the cross-examiner has been untruthful with his question and Lt. Kaffee failed to deal with this head on. If this ever happens, you must not shy away and instead relentlessly defend yourself until it is clear that the witness is the distorter. Here is an example:

> Q: *You just claimed that I distorted the truth of what happened during the unsanctioned punishment you gave Private Bell. The truth is that you ordered that Private Bell would receive no food or drink other than water for seven days, correct?*
>
> A: *Yes, but you didn't include the fact that he was given vitamin supplements.*
>
> Q: *Vitamin supplements aren't food are they?*
>
> A: *No.*
>
> Q: *And you ordered that all food and drink other than water be withheld from Private Bell for seven days because you wanted to cause him tremendous physical and mental pain, didn't you?*
>
> A: *Yes.*

The battle line is drawn. The witness attacked the cross-examiner's credibility for failing to include the vitamin supplements given to Private Bell. Given this witness's testimony thus far and the context of the allegation, I don't think he wins this one. But the most important point is that we must defend our credibility always, especially when it is under attack, and we have a rational defense.

The cross-examination goes on:

Q: Wouldn't this form of discipline be considered a Code Red?

A: Not necessarily.

Q: If I called the other eight thousand men at Guantanamo Bay to testify, would they consider it a Code Red?

Q: [Ross] Please the court, the witness can't possibly testify as to what eight thousand other men would say. We object to this entire line of questioning as argumentative and irrelevant badgering of the witness.

J: The government's objection is sustained, Lt. Kaffee, and I would remind you that you're now questioning a marine officer with an impeccable service record.

More of the same trouble for Lt. Kaffee, who fails to capitalize on the positive things the witness says and instead gets reprimanded by the judge. The main problem here is that Lt. Kaffee didn't understand how to deal with the "Not necessarily" answer. Let's examine how this could have been done differently:

Q: *How was your unauthorized barracks restriction depriving a man of everything except water and vitamin supplements for seven whole days different from a Code Red?*

I have no idea what the witness can say to make them different. While I don't know the answer to this question and am not 100 percent sure there is no answer that can hurt me, it is a calculated risk worth taking for a couple of reasons. First, the witness has already tried to differentiate the events and if I say nothing further then that is where it stands. Second, if he tries to make something up, I have something in my pocket waiting for him: Corporal Howard's previous testimony about receiving a Code Red where he was punched in the arm for five minutes and had glue poured on his hands.

Lt. Kaffee changed topics at this point:

Q: Lieutenant, was Dawson given a rating of Below Average on this last fitness report because you learned he'd been sneaking food to Private Bell?

A: Corporal Dawson was found to be Below Average because he committed a crime.

Q: What crime did he commit? Dawson brought a hungry guy some food. What crime did he commit?

A: He disobeyed an order.

Q: And because he did, because he exercised his own set of values, because he made a decision about the welfare of a marine that was in conflict with an order of yours, he was punished, is that right?

A: Corporal Dawson disobeyed an order.

Q: Yeah, but it wasn't an order, was it? After all, it's peacetime. He wasn't being asked to secure a hill or advance on a beachhead. I mean, surely a marine of Dawson's intelligence can be trusted to determine on his own which are the really important orders, and which orders might, say, be morally

questionable. Can he? Can Corporal Dawson determine on his own which orders he's gonna follow?

A: No, he cannot.

Q: A lesson he learned after the Curtis Bell incident,
am I right?

A: I would think so.

Q: You know so, don't you, Lieutenant?

Q: [Ross] Object!

J: Sustained.

Q: Lieutenant Kendrick, one final question: if you
ordered Dawson to give Santiago a Code Red—is it
reasonable to think that he would've disobeyed you
again?

A: I told those men not to touch Santiago.

There are a few problems here. First, Lt. Kaffee has
become too fixated on the point about whether Dawson
could refuse a Code Red order again and is not paying
enough attention to the main point of proving that Lt.
Kendrick ordered a Code Red on Private Santiago. Second,
the only question at the end that Lt. Kaffee devotes to
the main point is a bad question because it does not even
argue (through the witness) that Lt. Kendrick did order the
Code Red on Private Santiago per the word *if*. Let's examine how this could have been done better:

Q: *You previously said that you have never ordered a
Code Red?*

A: *Correct.*

Q: *You did order an unauthorized barracks restriction of Private Bell and deprived him of everything*

except water and vitamin supplements for seven whole days as punishment for stealing liquor from the officers' club?

A: Yes.

Q: *And you ordered Corporal Dawson to enforce this unauthorized punishment on Private Bell, didn't you?*

A: Yes.

Q: *And when Corporal Dawson disobeyed your order and gave Private Bell some food, you punished Corporal Dawson by rating him Below Average for the first time and keeping him from being promoted, didn't you?*

A: Yes.

Q: *So, you decided to inflict an unauthorized punishment on Private Bell for stealing liquor from the officers' club because you thought highly of him and didn't want to tarnish his record?*

A: Yes.

Q: *Yet, you then decided to tarnish the record of Corporal Dawson for bringing Private Bell some food and disobeying your order to inflict an unauthorized punishment on another marine?*

A: Yes.

Q: *Private Santiago was a Below Average marine who had also gone outside the chain of command, wasn't he?*

A: Yes.

Q: *Now, you claim that you never ordered any Code Red or other form of punishment on Private Santiago in spite of all this?*

A: *Correct. I explicitly ordered the men not to touch Private Santiago.*

Q: *Corporal Howard was physically punished for letting his weapon slip out of his hands and Private Bell was physically punished for stealing liquor from the officers' club, but Private Santiago was not physically punished for all of his subpar behavior and his breaking the chain of command?*

A: *No, he was not.*

While no one can say how the trier of fact would decide the outcome of this issue, I am confident that these are the right tools to make the best argument possible. The key is understanding what tools we have to demonstrate that the witness is untruthful.

The main problem here is that the witness publicly announced that no one was to touch Private Santiago and the only evidence of a contrary order is the defendant's claim that it was later given in private. While we don't have direct evidence to demonstrate that the witness is lying, we do have many tools available to diminish his credibility and enhance the odds that the trier of fact will agree with our version of events pursuant to the Rule of Probability.

Thus, this demonstrative cross-examination (and the pieces before it) has put together a mosaic of an untruthful witness who has ordered these types of physical punishments before and that Private Santiago's conduct fits that type of outcome. Using all of those tools and the power of their order and organization provide the greatest likelihood that the tier of fact will hear our answers instead of the witness's.

Captain Ross "cross-examines" for the prosecution:

Q: Lieutenant Kendrick, did you order Corporal Dawson and Private Downey to give Willy Santiago a Code Red?

A: No, I did not.

Q: Thank you.

Captain Ross correctly understands that this witness has been called by the defense to prove that Lt. Kendrick ordered the defendants to give Private Santiago a Code Red. Now Captain Ross cannot make everything OK because this witness made significant unforced errors that undermined his credibility and also possessed some structural problems that cannot be changed. However, this "cross-examination" does not identify all of the tools which are available to support the prosecution's theory of the case. Here's an example.

Q: *Lieutenant Kendrick, did you publicly order the entire platoon not to touch Private Santiago?*

A: *That's correct.*

Q: *Did you order everyone not to touch Private Santiago because your commanding officer, Colonel Jessup, ordered you to do that?*

A: *That's correct.*

Q: *Would you disobey a direct order from a superior officer?*

A: *No.*

Q: *Well, you previously didn't tell your commanding officer about Private Bell's punishment, what makes this different?*

A: *With Private Bell, I was not disobeying a direct order from a commanding officer. I was exercising my discretion to punish a marine informally so that his record wouldn't be tarnished. Disobeying a direct order not to punish someone is very different.*

Q: *Did you give a contrary order to the defendants in their room after the meeting when you announced that Private Santiago wasn't to be touched?*

A: *No, that never happened. I never went to their room, and I never issued any such order.*

Captain Ross's one question was not sufficient to help this witness and protect the prosecution's theory of the case. Given all the problems this witness has, the best (and maybe only good thing) he has is the public order and that there is no contrary evidence other than the defendant's claim. For the same reason that the defense must marshal all of their resources to attack this issue, the prosecution must do the same to protect it.

Private First Class Loudon Downey

The defense's third witness was one of the defendants, Private First Class Loudon Downey, who testified on direct examination in relevant part:

Q: Private, I want you to tell us one last time: Why did you go into Private Santiago's room on the night of September 6?

A: A Code Red was ordered by my platoon commander, Lt. Jonathan James Kendrick.

Q: Thank you.

The defense makes the significant decision to have one of the defendants testify. While the full direct examination transcript is not available, it is reasonable to assume that he testified that there was no intent to kill Private Santiago and denied putting poison on the rag. As anyone who has been in this position will tell you, putting a defendant on the stand is one of the most difficult trial decisions and generally only happens when the defense thinks they *must* do so to have a successful outcome.

This decision was probably necessary given how poorly this trial has gone for the defense thus far and since the defendants' statements are the only evidence of an order to give Private Santiago a Code Red against the contrary evidence of Lt. Kendrick's public order to the platoon not to touch Private Santiago.

Captain Ross cross-examines for the prosecution:

Q: Private, for the week of 2 September, the switch log has you down at Post 39 until 16:00, is that correct?
A: I'm sure it is, sir, they keep that log pretty good.
Q: How far is it from Post 39 to the Windward Barracks?
A: It's a ways, sir, it's a hike.
Q: About how far by jeep?
A: About ten, fifteen minutes, sir.
Q: Have you ever had to walk it?
A: Yes sir. That day, sir. Friday. The Pick-up Private— sir, that's what we call the fella who drops us at our posts and picks us up . . . also, cause he can get

girls in New York City—the Pick-up Private got a flat . . . Right at 39. He pulled up and blam! . . . A blowout, with no spare. We had to double-time it back to the barracks.

Q: And if it's ten or fifteen minutes by jeep, I'm guessing it must be a good hour by foot, am I right?

A: Pick-up and me did it in forty-five flat, sir.

Q: Not bad. Now you say your assault on Private Santiago was the result of an order that Lt. Kendrick gave in your barracks room at 16:20.

A: Yes, sir.

Q: But you just said that you didn't make it back to Windward Barracks until 16:45.

A: Sir?

Q: If you didn't make it back to your barracks until 16:45, then how could you be in your room at 16:20?

A: You see sir, there was a flat tire.

Q: Private, did you ever actually hear Lt. Kendrick order a Code Red?

A: No, sir.

Q: Why did you go into Santiago's room?

A: Hal? [The witness looks to the co-defendant for help.]

Q: Did Corporal Dawson tell you to do it? He did, didn't he? Dawson told you to give Santiago a Code Red.

A: Hal?

Q: Don't look at him.

A: Yes, Captain. I was given an order by my squad leader, Lance Corporal Harold W. Dawson of the US Marine Corps. And I followed it.

An interesting cross-examination indeed. Some readers may believe that Captain Ross has done a fine job with this. Captain Ross utilizes a series of controlled open-ended questions to discredit the defendant's testimony that Lt. Kendrick *directly* ordered him to give Private Santiago a Code Red. While this cross-examination was very well-executed within the boundaries of what it was intended to achieve, it is nevertheless an illustration of how something can look like a good idea, but in fact be a terrible mistake.

Captain Ross's last two questions buttress the defense's theory that a Code Red was the reason this happened instead of an intentional murder with a poisoned rag to keep Private Santiago from informing on Corporal Dawson. These questions simply do not make any sense given that both defendants are charged with Conspiracy to Commit Murder and Murder in the First Degree.

Indeed, these questions have not only allowed Private Downey to claim that he is innocent of the charges since he was ordered to give Private Santiago a Code Red by Corporal Dawson, but Captain Ross's last question actually suggests that idea to the defendant and supports the argument that this *was* in fact a Code Red! If true, Private Downey would thus be not guilty of Conspiracy to Commit Murder and Murder in the First Degree. Moreover, this could potentially jeopardize the charges against Corporal Dawson, as well, since it makes a mess of the entire prosecution case theory.

The important takeaway is that Captain Ross's disastrous last two questions have nothing to do with the form of the question, but instead his strategic failure to maintain a consistent theory of the case resulting in the question helping the defendant. Captain Ross thought that damaging

Private Downey's credibility by proving that he did not actually hear Lt. Kendrick's order was the important point to be made on the cross-examination. But it was not. Instead, damaging Private Downey's credibility is merely an important stepping stone in demonstrating the falsity of the defense's position and not an end unto itself. Captain Ross has unwittingly fallen into a trap of his own making.

We must also assume that Private Downey will at some point find a way to distinguish between hearing the actual order and getting it through the chain of command. Thus, Captain Ross needs to deal with this inevitable explanation and cannot leave it for later. Here is an alternative cross-examination picking up from the second-to-last question:

Q: *You testified on direct examination that "a Code Red was ordered by my platoon commander, Lt. Jonathan James Kendrick"?*

A: *Yes.*

Q: *That isn't true, you never heard him say any such thing, correct?*

A: *Well, I mean that the order came from him, but that I didn't hear it directly from him. Corporal Dawson told me that that we were ordered to do it by Lt. Kendrick.*

Q: *Now, Corporal Dawson never previously allowed any Code Reds to be given to Private Santiago, did he?*

A: *No, he didn't.*

Q: *In fact, you heard testimony that Corporal Dawson snuck food to PFC Bell when he was placed on barracks restriction by Lt. Kendrick with orders that he be denied food?*

A: Yes.

Q: Now, after refusing for some time to allow any-one to give Private Santiago a Code Red and going against Lt. Kendrick's order in helping PFC Bell, you now claim that Corporal Dawson delivered the order to give Private Santiago a Code Red?

A: Yes.

Q: And you claim that Corporal Dawson happened to give you this order on the same day you both found out that Private Santiago had informed on Corporal Dawson in alleging that Corporal Dawson had illegally fired into Cuba?

A: Yes.

Q: Now, if Corporal Dawson was found guilty of ille-gally firing into Cuba, he faced significant reper-cussions, didn't he?

A: Yes.

Q: And eliminating Private Santiago's eyewit-ness account was the only thing that could save Corporal Dawson from those significant repercus-sions, wasn't it?

A: No, we didn't intend to kill Private Santiago.

Q: So, on the same day that you both found out that Private Santiago was offering incriminating infor-mation against Corporal Dawson, you went to Private Santiago's room in the middle of the night?

A: Yes, we were ordered to give him a Code Red.

Q: You both found out that Private Santiago was offer-ing incriminating information against Corporal Dawson and went to his room in the middle of the night with a poison-laced rag and shoved it down his throat, didn't you?

A: *No, there was no poison, and we didn't intend to kill Private Santiago.*

Q: *You took that poison-laced rag, shoved it down his throat, and then duct taped his arms and legs together so that he couldn't remove the poison-laced rag, didn't you?*

A: *No, there was no poison, and we didn't intend to kill Private Santiago. We were ordered to give him a Code Red.*

You can, of course, judge the efficacy of this cross-examination. I myself don't know whether it is good enough to defeat Private Downey's defense that both men are innocent or even his potential argument that he is innocent as an unwitting pawn of Corporal Dawson. But that is, of course, not the point of the exercise, especially where we are dealing with cold transcript and can't make the full credibility analysis that live testimony offers.

That said, I am confident that this demonstrative cross-examination is better than the one Captain Ross put forth because the formulation of the questions stays in the theory of his case. And that is the whole point of cross-examination. It is the construct of the questions that are persuasive or not, with the witness's answers largely expected. The issue will be whether the witness's answers are believed. If the witness answers in accord with the questions, it is because doing so is better than the alternative. If the witness chooses to evade the questions, it will not matter to the trier of fact because they have heard the answer in their own heads and the witness's unresponsive answers will diminish their credibility.

Colonel Nathan R. Jessup

The defense's fourth witness was Colonel Nathan R. Jessup. While this is technically a direct examination, the witness is adverse to the defense so we will analyze it as a cross-examination, like we did with Lt. Kendrick.

Q: Colonel, when you learned of Santiago's letter to the NIS, you had a meeting with your two senior officers, is that right?

A: Yes.

Q: The platoon commander, Lt. Jonathan Kendrick, and the executive officer, Lt. Colonel Matthew Markinson.

A: Yes.

Q: And at present, Colonel Markinson is dead, is that right?

Q: [Ross] Objection. I'd like to know just what defense counsel is implying?

Q: I'm implying simply that, at present, Colonel Markinson is not alive.

Q: [Ross] Surely Colonel Jessup doesn't need to appear in this courtroom to confirm that information.

Q: I just wasn't sure if the witness was aware that two days ago, Colonel Markinson took his own life with a .45 caliber pistol.

J: The witness is aware, the Court is aware, and now the jury is aware. We thank you for bringing this to our attention. Move on, Lieutenant.

Q: Yes, sir. Colonel, at the time of this meeting, you gave Lt. Kendrick an order, is that right?

A: I told Kendrick to tell his men that Santiago wasn't to be touched.

Q: And did you give an order to Colonel Markinson as well?

A: I ordered Markinson to have Santiago transferred off the base immediately.

Lt. Kaffee uses two controlled open-ended questions to elicit the most important information in the examination, that no one should touch Private Santiago and that Private Santiago should be transferred off the base. These two pieces of information are critical because they are potentially at odds with each other, like an intellectual Mack Truck collision.

Q: Why?

A: I felt that his life might be in danger once word of the letter got out.

This is the issue that will make or break this cross-examination and the whole case. It is executed with a controlled opened-ended question that Lt. Kaffee thinks he knows the answer to, but there is another answer that could have hurt him.* Imagine instead if the witness had

---

* One could argue that the witness is locked into his answer since he has already taken this position in a previous meeting. However, the attendees of that meeting were the witness, Lt. Kaffee and his co-counsel, Lt. Kendrick, and a now deceased Colonel Markinson. As such, Lt. Kaffee has no evidence of the previous statement to control the witness if he deviates other than turning a member of the defense team into witnesses (and they weren't taking notes), or getting Lt. Kendrick to agree this was said (unlikely to happen). As such, we are dealing with this as though the witness is free to answer without prior constraint.

said, "He was being transferred off the base because this wasn't the right posting for him" or "He was being transferred off the base because he had requested a transfer and it was granted." If the witness had said something like this, then this whole thing likely falls apart.

However, given how poorly things have gone for the defense to this point, this was probably worth the gamble. As we have discussed, witnesses sometimes make mistakes, and we must capitalize on it when they do.

Lt. Kaffee goes on:

Q: Grave danger?

A: Is there another kind?

Q: We have the transfer order that you and Markinson co-signed, ordering that Santiago be lifted on a flight leaving Guantanamo at six the next morning. Was that the first flight off the bass?

A: The six a.m. flight was the first flight off the base.

Q: Colonel, you flew up to Washington early this morning, is that right?

A: Yes.

Q: I notice you're wearing your Class A appearance in dress uniform for court today.

A: As are you, Lieutenant.

Q: Did you wear that uniform on the plane?

Q: [Ross] Please the Court, is this dialogue relevant to anything in particular?

Q: The defense didn't have an opportunity to depose this witness, your honor. I'd ask the Court for a little latitude.

J: A very little latitude.

Q: Colonel?

A: I wore fatigues on the plane.

Q: And you brought your dress uniform with you.

A: Yes.

Q: And a toothbrush? A shaving kit? Change of underwear?

Q: [Ross] Your honor.

Q: Is the Colonel's underwear a matter of national security?

J: Gentlemen. You better get somewhere fast with this, Lieutenant.

Q: Yes, sir. Colonel?

A: I brought a change of clothes and some personal items.

Q: After Dawson and Downey's arrest on the night of the sixth, Santiago's barracks room was sealed off and its contents inventoried. Pairs of camouflage pants, six camouflage shirts, two pairs of boots, one pair of brown shoes, one pair of tennis shoes, eight khaki T-shirts, two belts, one sweater—

Q: [Ross] Please the Court, is there a question anywhere in our future?

J: Lt. Kaffee, I have to—

Q: I'm wondering why Santiago wasn't packed. I'll tell you what, we'll get back to that one in a minute. This is a record of all telephone calls made from your base in the past twenty-four hours. After being subpoenaed to Washington, you made three calls. I've highlighted those calls in yellow. Do you recognize those numbers?

A: I called Colonel Fitzhughes in Quantico, Virginia. I wanted to let him know I'd be in town. The second call was to set up a meeting with Congressman Richmond of the House Armed Services Committee, and the third call was to my sister Elizabeth.

Nine questions later, the judge is losing patience, and we are barely getting to the point. Lt. Kaffee only needs to ask one question to make his point. My advice is that people don't come to a baseball game to watch the windup: they come for the pitch.

Q: Why did you make that call, sir?
A: I thought she might like to have dinner tonight.
Q: [Ross] Judge—
J: I'm gonna put a stop to this now.
Q: Your honor, these are the telephone records from GITMO for September 6. And these are fourteen letters that Santiago wrote in nine months requesting, in fact begging, for a transfer. Upon hearing the news that he was finally getting his transfer, Santiago was so excited, that do you know how many people he called? Zero. Nobody. Not one call to his parents saying he was coming home.
Not one call to a friend saying 'can you pick me up at the airport.' He was asleep in his bed at midnight, and according to you he was getting on a plane in six hours, yet everything he owned was hanging neatly in his closet and folded neatly in his footlocker. You were leaving for one day and you packed a bag and made three phone calls. Santiago

was leaving for the rest of his life, and he hadn't called a soul and he hadn't packed a thing. Can you explain that? The fact is there was no transfer order. Santiago wasn't going anywhere, isn't that right, Colonel?

Q: [Ross] Object. Your Honor, it's obvious that Lt. Kaffee's intention this morning is to smear a high-ranking marine officer in the desperate hope that the mere appearance of impropriety will win him points with the jury. It's my recommendation, sir, that Lt. Kaffee receive an official reprimand from the bench, and that the witness be excused with the Court's deepest apologies.

J: Overruled.

Q: [Ross] Your honor—

J: The objection's noted.

Q: Colonel? Is this funny, sir?

A: No. It's not. It's tragic.

Q: Do you have an answer?

A: Absolutely. My answer is I don't have the first damn clue. Maybe he was an early morning riser, and he liked to pack in the night. And maybe he didn't have any friends. I'm an educated man, but I'm afraid I can't speak intelligently about the travel habits of William Santiago. What I do know is that he was set to leave the base at 0600. Now are these really the questions I was called here to answer? Phone calls and footlockers? Please tell me you've got something more, Lieutenant. Please tell me there's an ace up your sleeve. These two marines are on trial for their lives. Please tell me their lawyer hasn't pinned their hopes to a phone bill. Do you have any other questions for me, counselor?

Lt. Kaffee thought he had a great line of questioning, but didn't understand that he doesn't have the evidence or the Rule of Probability to prove that Private Santiago was never going to be transferred off the base. The witness had an easy answer to refute this line of questioning, and Lt. Kaffee is ignoring a better available strategy.

J: Lieutenant, do you have anything further for this witness?

A: Thanks, Danny. I love Washington. [stands up]

Q: Excuse me, I didn't dismiss you.

A: I beg your pardon.

Q: I'm not through with my examination. Sit down.

A: What would you like to discuss now. My favorite color?

Q: Colonel, the six a.m. flight was the first one off the base?

A: Yes.

Q: There wasn't a flight that left seven hours earlier and landed at Andrews Airforce Base at two a.m.?

J: Lieutenant, I think we've covered this, haven't we?

Q: Your Honor, these are the Tower Chief's Logs for both Guantanamo Bay and Andrews Airforce Base. The Guantanamo log lists no flight that left at eleven p.m., and the Andrews log lists no flight that landed at two a.m. I'd like to admit them as Defense Exhibits "A" and "B."

J: I don't understand. You're admitting evidence of a flight that never existed?

Q: We believe it did, sir. Defense'll be calling Airman Cecil O'Malley and Airman Anthony Perez. They were working the ground crew at Andrews at two a.m. on the seventh.

Q: [Ross] Your Honor, these men weren't on the list.

Q: Rebuttal witnesses, Your Honor, called specifically to refute testimony offered under direct examination.

While this may sound good, in reality, there is not actually any evidence or witnesses proving that there was an unlogged earlier flight leaving Guantanamo Bay for Andrews Airforce Base. Credibility is the coin of the realm. Never claim that you have evidence which doesn't actually exist. If the bluff gets called, the results will be catastrophic.

J: I'll allow the witnesses.

A: This is ridiculous.

Q: Colonel, a moment ago—

A: Check the Tower Logs, for Christ's sake.

Q: We'll get to the airmen in just a minute, sir. A moment ago you said that you ordered Kendrick to order his men not to touch Santiago.

A: That's right.

Q: And Kendrick was clear on what you wanted?

A: Crystal.

Q: Any chance Kendrick ignored the order?

A: Ignored the order?

Q: Any chance he just forgot about it?

A: No.

Q: Any chance Kendrick left your office and said, "The old man's wrong?"

A: No.

Q: When Kendrick spoke to the platoon and ordered them not to touch Santiago, any chance they ignored him?

A: Have you ever spent time in an infantry unit, son?

Q: No, sir.

A: Ever served in a forward area?

Q: No, sir.

A: Ever put your life in another man's hands, ask him to put his life in yours?

Q: No, sir.

A: We follow orders, son. We follow orders or people die. It's that simple. Are we clear?

Q: Yes, sir.

A: Are we clear?

Through the Looking Glass indeed. The witness has asked the cross-examiner five questions, which is five too many. If a witness suddenly asks the cross-examiner a question, the cross-examiner must swiftly Pull the Chain and bring reality back in order. Here's an example:

Q: *Colonel, the way things work in a courtroom is that I ask the questions and you are to answer them truthfully. Are you able to control yourself and follow these instructions?*

Cross-examiners ask the questions and witnesses answer them, not the other way around. If a witness crosses that line, you Pull the Chain hard. If they do it again, repeat with pleasure.

Lt. Kaffee continues:

Q: Crystal. Colonel, I have just one more question before I call Airman O'Malley and Airman Perez: If you gave an order that Santiago wasn't to be touched, and your orders are always followed, then why would he be in danger, why would it be necessary to transfer him off the base?

A: Private Santiago was a sub-standard marine. He was being transferred off the base because—

Finally, the question that matters. Once the witness previously said that Private Santiago was being transferred off the base for his own protection, it was game over. After all the previous gyrations, roads to nowhere, and posturing about fake witnesses, Lt. Kaffee has finally found the promised land. Better late than never.

Q: But that's not what you said. You said he was being transferred because he was in grave danger.

A: Yes. That's correct, but—

Let the witness answer the question, especially when they are drowning and making it worse for themselves.

Q: You said, "He was in danger." I said, "Grave danger." You said—

A: Yes, I recall what—

Q: I can have the Court Reporter read back your—

A: I know what I said. I don't need it read back to me like I'm a damn—

Q: Then why the two orders? Colonel? Why did you—

A: Sometimes men take matters into their own hands.

Q: No, sir. You made it clear just a moment ago that your men never take matters into their own hands. Your men follow orders or people die. So Santiago shouldn't have been in any danger at all, should he have, Colonel?

A: You little bastard.

The witness finally gets to give his answer, and Lt. Kaffee impeaches with the witness's prior statement, which keeps him from wiggling out of the box. It is fair to say that the cross-examiner is doing something right if the witness calls them a "little bastard."

Q: [Ross] Your Honor, I have to ask for a recess to—

Q: I'd like an answer to the question, Judge.

J: The Court'll wait for answer.

Q: If Kendrick told his men that Santiago wasn't to be touched, then why did he have to be transferred? Kendrick ordered the code red, didn't he? Because that's what you told Kendrick to do.

Q: [Ross] Object!

J: Counsel.

Q: And when it went bad, you cut these guys loose.

Q: [Ross] Your Honor—

J: That'll be all, counsel.

Q: You had Markinson sign a phony transfer order—
   you doctored the log books.
A: You want answers?

Back to the upside down world where the witness asks the
questions and the cross-examiner answers . . .

Q: I think I'm entitled to them.
A: You want answers?!
Q: I want the truth.
A: You can't handle the truth! Son, we live in a
   world that has walls. And those walls have to be
   guarded by men with guns. Who's gonna do it?
   You? You, Lt. Weinberg? I have a greater responsibility than you can possibly fathom. You weep
   for Santiago and you curse the marines. You have
   that luxury. You have the luxury of not knowing
   what I know: That Santiago's death, while tragic,
   probably saved lives. And my existence, while gro-
   tesque and incomprehensible to you, saves lives.
   You don't want the truth. Because deep down, in
   places you don't talk about at parties, you want
   me on that wall. You need me there. We use words
   like honor, code, loyalty . . . we use these words
   as the backbone to a life spent defending something. You use 'em as a punchline. I have neither
   the time nor the inclination to explain myself to a
   man who rises and sleeps under the blanket of the
   very freedom I provide, then questions the manner in which I provide it. I'd prefer you just said
   thank you and went on your way. Otherwise, I

suggest you pick up a weapon and stand a post.
Either way, I don't give a damn what you think
you're entitled to.

Q: Did you order the Code Red?

A: I did the job you sent me to do.

Q: Did you order the Code Red?

A: You're goddamn right I did.

A Hollywood ending if there ever was one. The bad guy
lies vanquished in the street, and the hero walks away tri-
umphantly. And that is all well and good for entertainment, but we are not here for entertainment. We are learning what works and what doesn't. Notwithstanding its
successful outcome, this "cross-examination" is largely an
example of what not to do.

Almost everything Lt. Kaffee did with this witness
was poorly executed. His questions were poor, he went
on rambling tangents, he lied to the Court about having
witnesses and evidence that he really didn't have, he put
his credibility on the line for something that didn't even
matter, and he allowed the witness to ask him a series of
questions.

The only good thing was when the witness put himself
into the intellectually impossible position of simultaneously claiming that Private Santiago was being transferred
off of the base for his safety and also claiming that the
order was given not to touch Private Santiago, which
would ensure his safety.

So what did Lt. Kaffee do right? He heard the witness.
Lt. Kaffee asked a question that had other answers that
could hurt him. But he got lucky and the witness made

a grave mistake in saying that the order was for Private Santiago's protection. But none of that would have mattered if Lt. Kaffee did not hear the witness and have the dexterity to take advantage of it. Once he realized what he had, he held on for dear life, Pulled the Chain, asked it again and again, and utilized his impeachment tool to keep the witness in an impossible position.

Summary

A Few Good Men is another well-regarded trial film. If you have seen it before, I am confident that you now see it differently after applying the strategy and tactics of cross-examination. Like *My Cousin Vinny*, the outcome of the case does not matter for our purposes. That said, it is only fair to know the result after analyzing the trial transcript.

The jury deliberated and found the defendants not guilty of the first two counts: Conspiracy to Commit Murder and Murder in the First Degree. The jury did, however, find the defendants guilty of Conduct Unbecoming a United States Marine. They were sentenced to time served and were dishonorably discharged from the United States Marines.

What really does matter to us is how the principles of cross-examination were utilized so that we can learn from the good and the bad. As we saw, Lt. Kaffee and Captain Ross are different from Mr. Gambini: their respective cross-examinations were poorly done. Both often missed the important points for things that did not matter, or even worse, did things that helped prove the other side's theory of the case.

When we strip out the theatrical ending, we see two cross-examiners who often did more harm to themselves than the other side could have. Lt. Kaffee's inability to deal with Dr. Stone about the poison would have likely resulted in the convictions of both defendants but for Colonel Jessup's climatic confession. That is, of course, balanced against Captain Ross's cross-examination of Private Downey, which seized defeat from the jaws of victory on the murder charges and maybe also threw the case against Corporal Downey into doubt as well. This is, of course, a non-exhaustive list of what we covered in the previous transcript analysis.

The reality is that no one plays the game perfectly in real life either. We don't get multiple takes, and we don't get the benefit of looking back and analyzing it like we do here. But the good news is that you don't have to be perfect. If you utilize these techniques, you will more likely be able to control the outcome of your contests.

CHAPTER TWENTY

The People of the State of Michigan vs. Lieutenant Frederick Manion

N ow for our third and final case study. As you no doubt assume given our previous cases, this one is also based upon a movie. It is, however, different from the others in a material respect: the film *Anatomy of a Murder* was based upon a book (of the same name) about a real case and it was written by the attorney who defended it.*

Notwithstanding the fact that our society has changed significantly since the 1950s, I have chosen this case study as the last one for good reason: it is the most sophisticated of them all. In order to fully appreciate the strategy and issues of this case, we needed to create the new muscles that come after learning the principles and analyzing the first two case studies.

---

* Robert Traver was the name of the author who wrote *Anatomy of a Murder*, but it was a pen name used by John D. Voelker, who became a Michigan Supreme Court justice. Moreover, the judge in the film is played by Joseph N. Welch, the lawyer who famously asked Senator Joseph McCarthy, "Have you no sense of decency, sir, at long last?"

Here is the background of the case. In 1958, Lieutenant Frederick Manion was charged with Murder in the State of Michigan, Court of Iron Cliffs. Lt. Manion shot Bernard ("Barney") Quill, a local barkeeper who Lt. Manion claimed had raped his wife, Laura Manion. There is no dispute that Lt. Manion shot and killed Mr. Quill. The issue for the jury was whether Lt. Manion was legally culpable for the killing or not.

The People were represented by Mitch Lodwick and Claude Dancer, and Lt. Manion was represented by Paul Biegler.

Dr. Raschid

The prosecution's first witness is Dr. Raschid, who is examined by Mitch Lodwick:

Q: Dr. Raschid, did you perform an autopsy on the body of one Barney Quill?

A: I did on the night of August 17th in the Saint Francis Hospital of this city.

Q: Were you able to determine the cause of death?

Q: [Biegler] The defense will accept a summary of the report.

Q: People agree, your honor.

J: The witness will state the necessary facts.

A: The body of Quill had sustained five gunshot wounds. One of the bullets had passed through the heart. Death, in my opinion, was almost instantaneous and was directly caused by this wound.

Q: May I have your detailed report? I ask that this report be marked People's Exhibit One for identification.[7]

Paul Biegler cross-examines for the defense:

Q: Dr. Raschid, your primary purpose was to ascertain the cause of death, was it not?
A: Yes
Q: And yet I see by your report that you checked to determine whether spermatogenesis was occurring in the body of the deceased at the time of death.
Q: [Lodwick] Objection, your honor. The People have called this witness only to show cause of death.
Q: Your Honor, the entire report was offered as evidence, and the report contains this information about spermatogenesis.
J: Overruled, Mr. Lodwick. The witness may answer.

Mr. Biegler's second question reveals that he does not intend to accept the narrow paradigm of the prosecution's case. Instead, the defense needs to demonstrate that the defendants wife was raped by Mr. Quill (or that he believed she had been) for the possibility of an acquittal. The prosecution objects in an effort to keep that information out of the trial.

The problem with this objection is that it had almost no chance of success, for two reasons. First, the spermatogenesis information was in the report that they moved into evidence. As such, it is unreasonable to preclude the other side from examining material that you put at issue.

Second, the larger question beyond the spermatogenesis is whether it is practicable for the prosecution to preclude the other side from making their defense. As we shall we, this is an unreasonable position, hurts the prosecution's ability to effectively deal with it, and diminishes their credibility.

> A: Yes, I made that examination on the deceased.
> Q: Will you tell the Court your findings?
> A: Spermatogenesis was occurring at the time of death.
> Q: In other words, the deceased, in life, was not sterile. He could produce children?
> A: That is correct.

Notice how Mr. Biegler never calls Mr. Quill "the victim." Instead, Mr. Biegler either uses his name or calls him "the deceased" because the ethos of his argument is that Laura Manion was the victim, not Mr. Quill.

> Q: Now, Doctor, if a woman says she's had intercourse with a certain man and this man is proved fertile, yet no evidence is found in the woman's body, couldn't a lawyer—say a prosecuting attorney—use this as evidence that the woman is lying?
> Q: [Lodwick] Your Honor, I object to this line of questioning. We are not concerned here with whether or not there's been relations between a man and a woman.
> Q: Since an examination for spermatogenesis was made, certainly we're entitled to know why.
> J: Objection overruled. You may answer.
> A: Yes, prosecution could use that, though certainly it would not be conclusive that she was lying.

Again the prosecution sees where this going, tries to stop it, and fails. Mr. Biegler now deftly uses the spermatogenesis analysis to support his defense theory and make the argument that nothing in the report undermines Mrs. Manion's claim that she was raped by Mr. Quill.

> Q: Why not?
> A: Well, there could be several reasons why the test on her was negative. The use of a contraceptive or possibly there was no completion on the part of the man.

A brilliant controlled open-ended question by Mr. Biegler because no answer can hurt him. Given his previous answer, the witness is going to say something that explains why Mrs. Manion could have been raped by Mr. Quill with no presence of spermatogenesis.

> Q: In this post-mortem, were you also asked to determine whether or not the deceased had reached sexual climax shortly before his death?
> A: No, sir.
> Q: Could you have made such a determination?
> A: Oh yes.

Two more controlled open-ended questions aimed straight at the prosecution's credibility.

> Q: Then you were only asked to make such examination as might be useful to the prosecution, but none which might help the defense?

Q: [Claude Dancer] I object, your Honor. The question is argumentative. Counsel for the defense is trying to impugn the integrity of the representatives of the People.

J: Mr. Biegler, you must be aware that the question is improper.

Q: I withdraw the question and apologize.

J: The question and answer will be stricken and the jury will disregard both the question and the answer.

Q: That's all the questions I have.

Q: [Lodwick] No re-direct.

A seemingly rudimentary witness to establish the undebatable truth that Mr. Quill was shot five times and killed becomes anything but. The defense effectively seizes the opportunity to implement the Hitchhiking and Limiting techniques, uses the witness as a vehicle to begin putting in its theory of defense, and diminishes the prosecution's credibility. So begins the case within the case.

Lloyd Burke

The prosecution's second witness was Lloyd Burke, who was examined by Mitch Lodwick:

Q: Will you state your profession please, Mr. Burke?

A: I'm a commercial photographer.

Q: Were you called upon by the police to take photographs of the body of the deceased Bernard Quill before and after he was removed from the scene?

A: Yes, sir, I was.

Q: Were these the photographs of the deceased made by you?

A: They were.

Q: The reporter will please mark these photographs People's Exhibit 282D for identification. Photographs are tendered to the defense for examination and the People move their admission as evidence. Your witness.

Q: [Biegler] No questions and no objection. [pauses] Just a moment Mr. Burke. These photographs offered as evidence, are they the only photographs you took that night?

A: No.

Q: I suppose the others didn't turn out, is that it?

A: All my pictures turn out.

There is no reason to attack the credibility of this witness since he does not decide what pictures are turned over or presented at trial. Indeed, this is a Hitchhiking witness, and the tone of questioning should be consistent with the principle that he has helpful information that the prosecution (not the witness) did not want introduced.

Q: Well, of course. I beg your pardon. Did you give the other photographs to the police?

A: Yes sir, I did.

Q: Well, Mr. Burke, what were they? Were they side shots, or a shot of the moon perhaps, or a black bear scavenging the Thunder Bay dump?

Q: [Lodwick] Your Honor, I object. The photographs in evidence were introduced to show that the deceased met with a violent death.

Q: Your Honor, I should think that any photographs pertaining to the case would be relevant.

J: The point is good, Mr. Biegler. You may continue.

Mr. Biegler finally gets with the Hitchhiking program and is able to hurt the prosecution's credibility. Even better, the prosecution futilely objects, which indicates they don't want the jury to see or hear the information.

Q: What were the other photographs of, Mr. Burke?

A: Lieutenant Manion's wife.

Q: You mean these photographs show how she looked on that night after Barney Quill was killed?

Q: [Dancer] Your Honor, how Mrs. Manion looked is irrelevant. No evidence has been introduced to connect Mrs. Manion's appearance to the charge of murder.

J: Sustained.

Q: I'm sorry, your Honor. I wanted to be sure that the prosecution was not withholding evidence.

Q: [Lodwick] Now look here! I protest. The defense attorney's persistent attack on the motives of the prosecution . . .

J: The jury will disregard the remark made by the attorney for the defense. There's no reason to believe that the prosecution has not acted in good faith.

Q: My apologies to the prosecution and the Court. But your Honor, as long as protests are being made, I would like to protest myself. Now I'm perfectly willing to take on these two legal giants any time, any place, but in common fairness it ought to be one at a time. I don't want them pitching knuckle-balls at me at the same time.

J: It seems to me that you're batting close to a thousand with a bat in each hand, but your point is well taken. Whichever attorney opens with the witness, he alone shall continue with that witness until that witness is excused.

Q: Thank you, your Honor. No more questions.

Q: [Lodwick] No questions.

Another interesting cross-examination from Mr. Biegler. His initial view was not to ask any questions of the witness since the pictures of Mr. Quill's body were the only thing elicited. He then changed his mind and decided to cross-examine to show there were pictures of Mrs. Manion's physical condition and that they were not disclosed.

The issue with this cross-examination is that Mr. Biegler goes too far in explicitly attacking the motives of the prosecution, which earned him a stern rebuke from the judge, who then gave a vote of confidence to the prosecution. Mr. Biegler went too far because he doesn't have a basis to claim that the prosecution committed intentional wrongdoing and that damages his own credibility instead of theirs.

The point that Mr. Biegler should make is that Mrs. Manion's face was bruised on the night of the shooting, which lends strong credibility to the claim that she was attacked. Instead of doing this as a direct attack against the prosecution's credibility, he would have been better served by simply asking the question that really mattered. For example:

Q: What were the other photographs of, Mr. Burke?

A: Lieutenant Manion's wife.

Q: You mean these photographs show how she looked on that night after Barney Quill was killed?

Q: *Did your photographs of Mrs. Manion capture the bruises and swelling on her face?*

Now the prosecution would probably have again objected, but Mr. Biegler would have made his point if he asked the question this way. He may even have escaped the judge's wrath and the subsequent statement supporting the prosecution's credibility. The real damage to the prosecution's credibility will occur if and when the details of her rape allegation are made and the trier of fact recalls the prosecution's efforts to keep evidence of it from them.

Alphonse Paquette

The prosecution's third witness was Alphonse Paquette, who was examined by Mitch Lodwick:

Q: Would you state your name, please?

A: Alphonse Paquette.

Q: You work at the Thunder Bay Inn, don't you, Mr. Paquette?

A: I'm bartender there.

Q: Were you working on the night that Barney Quill was shot by Frederick Manion?

A: I was.

Q: Were you witness to the shooting?

A: I was.

Q: Please tell us in your own words what happened.

A: I was at a table by the door when Lieutenant Manion came in.

Q: Did you know Lieutenant Manion by sight and by name?

A: Yes, sir.

Q: Go ahead.

A: Well, he came in, walked over to the bar, and began to shoot. He shot Barney when he came up to the bar and when Barney fell, he kept on shooting down at Barney behind the bar. Then he turned around and walked out.

Q: When Lieutenant Manion entered the bar, how did he appear to you?

A: Well, he walked slow, kind of deliberate I guess you'd say.

Q: Did he speak to Barney Quill?

A: Not a word. He just walked over and pulled out his gun and bang!

Q: Then he walked out?

A: Yes.

Q: As he walked out, how did he appear to you?

A: Seemed just like he did when he walked in. Like he was the mailman. Delivering the mail.

Q: When Lieutenant Manion walked out of the bar, what did you do?

A: Well, it happened so fast, I guess I was stunned. Then I ran out after him.

Q: Did you find him outside?

A: Yes, sir, he was walking away.

Q: Did you speak to him?

A: Yes, sir, I said, "Lieutenant, you'd better not run away from this."

Q: Did he reply to you?

A: He said, "Do you want some too, buster?"

Q: Was he pointing the gun at you?

A: Well, he was holding the gun in my direction but the muzzle was low.

Q: When he said, "Do you want some too, buster," how was that expressed? Did he shout it? Was it hysterical? Was he hoarse? Did his voice tremble?

A: No, sir, he just said it cool and hard and looked right at me.

Q: Did he look to you, as far as you could tell, to be in complete possession of his faculties?

A: As far as I could tell.

Q: Your witness.

Mr. Biegler cross-examines for the defense:

Q: Mr. Paquette, did you see Laura Manion, wife of Lieutenant Manion, in the bar that night?

Q: [Lodwick] Your Honor, there he goes again. This is immaterial and irrelevant.

Q: The prosecution seems to be excessively jumpy, your Honor. I haven't gone anywhere yet.

J: Let's see where he is going before we object, Mr. Lodwick. Proceed, Mr. Biegler.

The prosecution is again trying to keep the defense from arguing their case, but this position is untenable. This is a prime example where following Sammy's Rule hurts the advocate's credibility. Instead of trying to futilely excise something, the prosecution should instead be figuring out how to steer into the skid and deal with it.

Q: Did you see Mrs. Manion in the bar?
A: She was there.
Q: Did you know when she left?
A: I don't remember when, but she left sometime.
Q: Did Barney Quill leave the bar that night?
A: Yes.
Q: How long was he gone?
A: I don't know exactly.

This line of questioning is poor. As usual, it is not the form of the questions, but the substance of them. Mr. Biegler is playing it too cute and doesn't make the principle point: that Mrs. Manion and Mr. Quill left the bar together.

Q: Do you remember when he returned?
A: I think he came back around midnight.
Q: Did you see him enter the bar?
A: Yes.
Q: From which entrance did he come? From the lobby entrance or the outside entrance?
A: It was from the lobby.

Q: How did he appear to you at the time?

A: How do you mean?

Q: Well, you understood the prosecuting attorney very well when he asked you that question about Lieutenant Manion's appearance.

A: Oh well, he was just old Barney, like usual.

An excellent use of Pulling the Chain. Not only does Mr. Biegler demonstrate that the witness is being evasive, but his question is structured to argue that the witness is biased since everyone appreciates the notion of "what is good for the goose is good for the gander."

While an excellent use of Pulling the Chain to attack the witness's credibility, this is also an example of how witnesses will make unforced errors. Frankly, this line of cross-examination was really going nowhere significant and the only positive moment was the witness's evasion. At least Mr. Biegler heard the witness and was able to make something out of nothing.

Q: Sober, reliable, gentle, salt-of-the-earth, friend-to-man Barney?

Q: [Lodwick] Your Honor, what kind of question is that?

Q: I withdraw the question, your Honor. Now, Mr. Paquette, had Barney changed his clothes since he left the bar?

It is usually advisable to wait until the judge has ruled on the objection before moving on. Assuming that the judge gave Mr. Biegler a look of disapproval, which is tantamount to being ruled against, then it is wise to tack away from the storm.

> **A:** I don't remember.
> **Q:** Might his clothes have been different when he returned? That is, might he have changed his clothes?
> **A:** I couldn't say. I didn't notice.

Mr. Biegler has asked an important question two times and each time, he has gotten an equivocation. When a witness sees the opportunity to safely equivocate and there is no mechanism to show they are being evasive, we can then use that equivocation against them with the Limiting technique. For example:

> **Q:** *So Mr. Paquette, it is possible that after leaving the bar with Mrs. Manion, Mr. Quill returned wearing different clothes?*

Thus, the witness has put himself into the position of having to agree that it was possible since his previous position is that he didn't know one way or the other.

> **Q:** Was Barney drinking that night?
> **A:** Well, he always had a few shots while he was talking to the customers. He was friendly.
> **Q:** Good old Barney. Now how many shots would you say good old Barney usually had?
> **A:** I don't know exactly.

Q: Wasn't he, in fact, pretty loaded that night, Mr. Paquette?

Q: [Lodwick] Objection, your Honor. If the deceased was dead drunk, it's no defense to this charge.

J: Sustained. I suggest you get off this, Mr. Biegler.

Another line of questioning where Mr. Biegler doesn't have either evidence or the Rule of Probability to force the witness to give him what he wants. And this time the witness doesn't make an unforced error like before. Mr. Biegler should have instead again used the witness's equivocation with the Limiting technique to argue it was possible that Mr. Quill had a lot to drink that night.

Q: Mr. Paquette, what do you call a man who has an insatiable penchant for women?

A: A what?

Q: A penchant, a desire, a taste, passion.

A: Well, a ladies man, I guess, or maybe just a damned fool.

J: Just answer the question, Mr. Paquette. The attorneys will provide the wisecracks.

Q: What else would you call a man like that, Mr. Paquette?

Q: [Lodwick] We can't see the drift of this, your Honor.

Q: You mean you do see it, Mr. Lodwick.

J: You may answer.

Q: Can you think of another name, Mr. Paquette?

A: Woman chaser?

Q: Try again.

A: Masher?

Q: Come now, Mr. Paquette, mashers went out with whalebone corsets and hairnets. Did you ever hear the expression wolf?

A: Sure. I've heard that. lt just slipped my mind.

Q: It slipped your mind. Well, naturally it would, clanking around in there with all those rusty old mashers. Have you ever known a man whom you could call a wolf, Mr. Paquette?

A: I'm not sure.

Q: Was Barney Quill a wolf, Mr. Paquette?

A: I couldn't say.

Q: Or wouldn't?

Q: [Lodwick] Objection.

J: Sustained. The question was answered, he couldn't say.

Another line of questioning where Mr. Biegler simply doesn't have the evidence or the Rule of Probability to get to where he wants to go. Frankly, Mr. Biegler is lucky to have gotten the equivocation from the witness since he did not have any ability to support his argument that Mr. Quill was a known predator.

Q: Mr. Paquette, when Barney returned from wherever he had gone, did he relieve you at the bar?

A: Yes, sir.

Q: And what did he say to you when he relieved you?

A: He said, "I'll take over."

Q: And when you came out from behind the bar, where did you go?

A: I went over to the table where the Pattersons were sitting.

Q: Now you testified that you were by the door when Lieutenant Manion came in. Is that the reason you were by the door, because the Pattersons' table was there?

A: Yes.

Q: Uh-huh. And how long was it before Lieutenant Manion came in?

A: I don't know, exactly, maybe thirty minutes.

Q: And you remained at the Pattersons' table all that time?

A: Yes, they're friends of mine.

Q: Is there also a window beside that table?

A: I think so.

Q: You think so. How long have you worked at the Thunder Bay Inn, Mr. Paquette?

A: Six or seven years.

Q: Well now, does this window by the table, does it suddenly vanish and reappear and come and go in a ghostly fashion?

A: It's there all the time.

Q: And when you looked out of the window, were you looking for something special?

A: No, I wasn't looking for anything.

Q: Didn't Barney Quill tell you to go over to that window and look out for Lieutenant Manion? Did he tell you to look out for Lieutenant Manion?

A: He did not.

If this is starting to feel like a familiar theme on this cross-examination, it is for good reason. Mr. Biegler has pursued numerous lines of questioning where he doesn't have the ability to make the point. Now Mr. Biegler has haphazardly pursued a line of questioning accusing the witness of being Mr. Quill's lookout for Lt. Manion. The witness was, of course, going to deny this, and Mr. Biegler has nothing to refute it. In the end, Mr. Biegler picked a fight that had no chance of success.

> Q: Mr. Paquette, Barney was quite a marksman, wasn't he? With guns? He'd won a lot of prizes for shooting, hadn't he?
>
> A: Yes.
>
> Q: Did he keep any guns behind the bar?
>
> A: He might have.
>
> Q: Isn't it a fact that there are three concealed pistol racks behind the bar, Mr. Paquette?
>
> Q: [Lodwick] Your honor, the defendant's plea is one of insanity, not self-defense.
>
> J: I'm sure Mr. Biegler hasn't forgotten that fact, Mr. Lodwick. You may answer.
>
> Q: Are there concealed gun racks behind the bar?
>
> A: Yes.
>
> Q: And how many people know about these gun racks?
>
> A: I couldn't say.
>
> Q: Now, isn't it a fact that once in a while Barney would take guns out of these racks and, twirling them on his finger, he'd demonstrate his skill to the patrons, isn't that—

A: I don't remember.

Q: Oh, now come on. Try and remember. Didn't you ever see him do that yourself?

A: Once or twice he did.

Q: That's all, Mr. Paquette. No further questions.

Another bad line of questioning only salvaged by the witness's decision to be evasive about something that did not matter. In the end, the consistent theme of this cross-examination is Mr. Biegler trying to fish without any bait. The fact that these things don't affect the outcome of the case only adds insult to injury. Let's take them in turn.

The points Mr. Biegler wanted to make were as follows: 1) that Mrs. Manion and Mr. Quill left the bar together; 2) that Mr. Quill changed his clothes between the time he left and came back; 3) that Mr. Quill was drunk; 4) that Mr. Quill preyed on women; 5) that Mr. Quill asked the witness to be his lookout for Lt. Manion; and 6) that Mr. Quill had guns at the bar and knew how to use them.

The sum total of these points amounts to a spaghetti-against-the-wall exercise to see what sticks. Mr. Biegler either failed to ask the relevant question or didn't have the goods to compel the answers. The result is damage to his credibility in the pursuit of unattainable goals.

To make matters worse, there were other areas that Mr. Biegler should have pursued instead of these dry holes. The problem goes back to understanding what technique to use on a witness. This witness does not fall into the Credibility Attack bucket, but he does fall into the

Hitchhiking and Limiting ones. Let's examine how this could have been done differently:

Q: *Lt. Manion walked into the bar, didn't he?*

A: *Yes.*

Q: *And he not only didn't run in, but he walked in slowly, didn't he?*

A: *Yes.*

Q: *You said on direct examination that Lt. Manion also walked out of the bar after shooting Mr. Quill?*

A: *Yes.*

Q: *So, after shooting a man five times in front of a bar full of people, he didn't run out, did he?*

A: *No, he walked out.*

Q: *And you described Lt. Manion as being like a mailman delivering the mail, didn't you?*

A: *Yes.*

Q: *So, after hearing that his wife was raped, Lt. Manion slowly walked into a bar full of people who knew him, calmly shot Mr. Quill five times, and then walked out like an emotionless mailman?*

A: *Well, I don't know anything about his wife being raped, but the rest of that is right.*

Q: *You said on direct that Lt. Manion looked like he was in full control of his faculties?*

A: *Yes.*

Q: *You're not a doctor?*

A: *No.*

Q: *You're not a close personal friend of Lt. Manion, are you?*

A: *No.*

> **Q:** *Given that you are not a doctor and don't even know him very well, you're not in a good position to evaluate his frame of mind, are you?*
>
> **A:** *I can just tell you my opinion based on what I saw.*
>
> **Q:** *Mr. Paquette, you're not in a position of giving this jury a clinical opinion about Lt. Manion's mental state, are you?*
>
> **A:** *No, I'm not.*

This cross-examination focuses on what matters to the case and what was possible to accomplish: whether or not Lt. Manion was in control of his faculties when he shot Mr. Quill. Mr. Parquette said very important things on direct examination, one which helped and two which hurt. The one that helped was the testimony about the mailman delivering the mail, and the two that hurt were the testimony that Lt. Manion appeared in control of his faculties and his statement after the shooting. Thus, these are the areas to Hitchhike and to Limit.

Mr. Paquette also claimed on direct examination that the defendant said, "Do you want some too, buster?" This claim also supports the theory that the defendant was in control of his faculties. I did not include this issue in the hypothetical cross-examination because there was no clear way to use any of our techniques against it. When we are confronted with such a situation, the best thing to do is to focus on the things we can deal with rather than make something worse by damaging our credibility with an empty argument.

George Lemon

The prosecution's fourth witness was George Lemon, and he was examined by Mitch Lodwick:

Q: Will you state your name, please?

A: George Lemon.

Q: What kind of work do you do, Mr. Lemon?

A: I'm caretaker of the tourist park at Thunder Bay. I see the place is clean and orderly. I check people in, check 'em out, and lock the gate at night.

Q: And what is your authority for these duties?

A: I'm paid by Masselin Township, and I'm also a deputy sheriff, just courtesy, sort of.

Q: Did you see Lieutenant Manion on the night of the fifteenth, the night Barney Quill was killed?

A: Yes, sir.

Q: Will you tell the court about how and when you saw Lieutenant Manion?

A: About 1 a.m., a knock on my door wakes me up. I went to the door and Lieutenant Manion was standing there. He said, "You better take me, Mr. Lemon, because I just shot Barney Quill." I told him to go back to his trailer and that I would call the State Police.

Q: How did Lieutenant Manion appear to you when he asked you to take him?

A: He said what he had to say and did what I told him. There wasn't any fuss.

Q: Did he appear to be, as far as you could tell, in complete possession of his faculties?

A: As far as I could tell, yes, sir.

Mr. Biegler cross-examines for the defense:

Q: Mr. Lemon, did you go to the Manions' trailer?

A: Yes, sir.

Q: Did you see Mrs. Manion at the trailer?

A: Yes, sir.

Q: What was her appearance?

A: She was a mess.

Q: [Lodwick] Objection; no evidence has been introduced to make Mrs. Manion's appearance relevant to this case.

Q: Well, no evidence has been introduced to make Barney Quill's appearance relevant, but you didn't object to the question then. Is that because you know that Barney Quill bathed and changed and cooled off after he raped and beat the hell out of this poor woman?

Q: [Lodwick] Your Honor, everybody in this court is being tried except Frederick Manion. I must protest—

Q: Now listen, this is a cross examination in a murder case, not a high-school debate. What are you and Dancer trying to do, railroad this soldier into the klink?

J: Mr. Biegler, you are an experienced attorney, and you know better than to make such an outburst. I will not tolerate intemperance of this sort. If you once again try the patience of this court, I shall hold you in contempt.

Q: Your Honor, I apologize; it won't happen again.

J: The witness's answer will be stricken and the jury will disregard the answer. Now you may proceed, Mr. Biegler.

I am of two minds about this issue. On the one hand, Mr. Biegler's outburst and statement in front of the jury is completely inappropriate. On the other hand, this may have been the irresistible impulse of an advocate being hamstrung in making his defense. The important point is that this should never be done intentionally and when the judge threatens you with contempt, you have no strikes left to give before you're out of there.

Q: Mr. Lemon, on the night when Lieutenant Manion awakened you and turned himself in, had you been awakened before, had anything else disturbed your slumbers?

A: No, sir.

Q: There were no soldiers singing?

A: No sir, not in my park after ten o'clock.

Q: There were no women screaming?

A: Well, those screams were down by the gate.

Q: [Lodwick] Objection, objection—

J: I see no reason for objecting yet, Mr. Lodwick.

Q: Tell us about those screams, Mr. Lemon.

A: I didn't hear 'em myself. There were some tourists in the park from Ohio, and they told me about them the next day.

J: Now, Mr. Lodwick.

Q: [Lodwick] This testimony is incompetent, hearsay, irrelevant, immaterial, inconclusive—

Q: Well, that's too much for me. The witness is yours.

Q: [Lodwick] Uh, no questions.

Mr. Biegler does better here, but he still leaves food on the plate. Like his cross-examination of Mr. Paquette, Mr. Biegler is myopically focused on proving the rape, but forgets that proving Lt. Manion's state of mind is a necessary element. It is certainly necessary for the trier of fact to believe that Mrs. Manion was raped (or that Lt. Manion honestly believed it to be true) to find that he had lost control of his faculties. But establishing the conditions for losing control of his faculties is not the end of it.

The trier of fact must believe that the defendant's conduct evidences the loss of control. This witness on direct examination rendered a lay opinion about Lt. Manion's mental state (like Mr. Paquette did), which was contrary to the defense's theory of the case. Here is an example of how to deal with it using the Limiting technique:

Q: *Mr. Lemon, you testified on direct examination that you thought that Lt. Manion was "in complete possession of his faculties" when you saw him?*

A: *Yes.*

Q: *Now, Mr. Lemon, you're not a doctor, are you?*

A: *No, I'm not.*

Q: *And you don't know Lt. Manion very well, do you?*

A: *No, I don't.*

Q: *And you didn't observe Lt. Manion before, during, or right after he shot Mr. Quill, did you?*

A: *No, I only saw him when he came to my place at Thunder Bay.*

Q: *And when he came to your place, he did so voluntarily and did exactly what you said to do?*

A: *Yes.*

Q: *He didn't try to run?*

A: *No.*

Q: *Mr. Lemon, you're not in a position of giving this jury a clinical opinion about Lt. Manion's mental state, are you?*

A: *No, I'm not.*

Thus, the name of the game is to use the good things the witness has to offer; in other words, that Lt. Manion was cooperative, and thereby limit the harmful layman's view that Lt. Manion was of sound mind when he shot Mr. Quill.

Detective Sergeant James Dirgo

The prosecution's fifth witness was Detective Sergeant James Dirgo and he was examined by Mitch Lodwick:

Q: State your name and occupation please.

A: Detective Sergeant James Dirgo, State Police.

Q: Were you called to Thunder Bay by Deputy Sheriff Lemon of Thunder Bay on the night that Barney Quill was shot and killed?

A: Yes, sir, I was. My companion officer and I were the first to be called in on the case.

Q: Sergeant Dirgo, when you arrived at the Manion trailer, who was there?

A: Lieutenant Manion and his wife were there.

Q: What did Lieutenant Manion say to you?

A: He said that his wife had had some trouble with Barney Quill; that he had gone to the tavern and shot Quill. He asked us whether Quill was dead or not. We told him he was.

Q: How did Lieutenant Manion take this information?

A: He didn't seem surprised.

Q: What did you do then, Sergeant Dirgo?

A: I asked for the gun he'd used.

Q: Did you take Lieutenant Manion down to the county jail here in Iron City that same night?

A: Yes, sir, we drove the Lieutenant down with his wife.

Q: On the drive to Iron City, did the Lieutenant talk further about the shooting?

A: He remarked that if he had the whole thing to do over again, he'd still do it.

Q: During all this at the trailer, the drive to Iron City, how did Lieutenant Manion appear to you?

A: He was very quiet, most of the time, seemed clearheaded.

Q: As far as you could tell, would you say that he was in complete possession of his faculties?

A: Seemed so to me.

Mr. Biegler cross-examines for the defense:

Q: Sergeant Dirgo, you testified that Lt. Manion told you that he shot Barney Quill after he learned that his wife had had "some trouble" with Quill. Now were these the words Lt. Manion used, "Some trouble"?

A: No, sir; those were my words, not his.

The opening that Mr. Biegler has been hoping for and the prosecution has served it up on a silver platter. Not only did they open the door to the topic they desperately want to keep out of the trial, but the prosecution also damaged their own credibility through a half-baked scheme to have their cake and eat it too.

> **Q:** And was it your notion to come here and use your own words?
> **A:** No, sir, it was not.
> **Q:** And was the suggestion to call it "some trouble" made by somebody here in this courtroom?
> **A:** Yes, sir, it was.

We can see that Mr. Biegler is hunting the credibility of his opposing counsel. Unfortunately, he lets the prosecutor off the hook by not going all the way.

> **Q:** All right, sergeant, now would you tell the court what words Lieutenant Manion actually used to describe the trouble his wife had had?
> **Q:** [Lodwick] Objection, your Honor. We've been over this before. This information would not be relevant to any issues before the court.
> **Q:** Now this statement concerning "some trouble" was brought out during the direct examination of Sergeant Dirgo. Up to now, you've adroitly restricted all testimony as far as Laura Manion's concerned; all right the cat's out of the bag, it's fair game for me to chase it.

J: This is a sore point, Mr. Biegler, and it's getting sorer. I'd like to hear from the prosecution.

Q: [Lodwick] The burden is on the defense to prove temporary insanity at the time of the shooting. Now if the reason for the alleged insanity is important to this case, then that is a matter for a competent witness, an expert on the subject of the human mind. What the defense is trying to do is introduce some sensational material for the purposes of obscuring the real issues.

Q: Your honor, how can the jury accurately estimate the testimony being given here unless they first know the reason behind this whole trial—why Lieutenant Manion shot Barney Quill. Now the prosecution would like to separate the motive from the act. Well, that's like trying to take the core from an apple without breaking the skin. The core of our defense is that the defendant's temporary insanity was triggered by this so-called trouble with Quill, and I beg the court, I beg the court to let me cut into the apple.

Q: [Lodwick] Our objection still stands, your Honor.

J: Objection overruled.

Mr. Biegler is now in business. The irony is that this may not have been possible had the prosecution not called this witness to the stand and elicited the defendant's statements. Calling this witness was a terrible mistake by the prosecution because the only substantive value he offered was the defendant's statements that he would do it again and that the witness thought he was in control of his faculties (which

two others have already said), which were highly out-
weighed by the negatives. Focusing on the good and ignoring the bad is the tell-tale sign of an advocate who cannot
view the case without their emotional thumb on the scale.

> Q: Sergeant Dirgo, tell the court how Lieutenant
> Manion described the trouble his wife had with
> Barney Quill.
> A: He told us that Quill had raped his wife.
> Q: Now can you recall generally what Lieutenant
> Manion told you about this rape?
> A: Yes, sir. He said he'd been asleep since right after
> dinner. He was woken up by some noise—screams,
> he thought, he got up, opened the trailer door, and
> went outside. His wife came running out of the
> dark and fell into his arms.
> Q: You saw his wife in the trailer. How'd she look?
> A: She was a little hysterical. She'd been pretty badly
> beaten up. She had big black bruises over her face
> and her arms.

Mr. Biegler is doing well, but he could be doing even better by digging deeper into the bruises, which are the best
evidence that Mrs. Manion was attacked. Indeed, the evidence is so powerful that the only reasonable way to counter it is to claim that the defendant instead caused them.
That is why more detail needs to be elicited to show that
these injuries were the result of a significant attack.

> Q: Did Mrs. Manion tell you about this rape and
> beating?

A: She did.

Q: And did she take you to the place where it happened?

A: Yes, sir, the next morning.

Q: And did you find anything there—any kind of evidence pertaining to the story Mrs. Manion had told you?

A: On the lane in the woods, we found some tire tracks and some dog tracks, and a leather case with some horn rim glasses inside. We also looked for a certain undergarment of Mrs. Manion's, but we didn't find it.

Q: Did you give Mrs. Manion a lie-detector test?

Q: [Lodwick] Objection. A polygraph test is inadmissible in our courts.

Q: I only asked if he gave the test; I didn't ask for the results.

J: He may answer that.

A: I gave her a lie detector test at her request.

Q: Now after all this investigation, did you believe Mrs. Manion?

A: I did.

Q: Even after the lie detector test?

Q: [Lodwick] Your Honor, I object to that question. It constitutes flagrant sneaking subterfuge on the part of the defense counsel.

J: Objection sustained. Ladies and gentlemen of the jury, a polygraph or lie detector test is not admissible into evidence, because nobody has ever been quite sure if some people couldn't lie to a lie detector and get away with it. Go ahead, Mr. Biegler.

Mr. Biegler was able to take the lie detector test point further than he probably should have been able to. However,
he got greedy by going too far with it, and the judge
decided to even out the playing field. The lesson is that
permission for a camel's nose under the tent is not a full
invitation.

> Q: In any case, Sergeant Dirgo, you yourself, in your
> own heart and mind, are quite convinced of Mrs.
> Manion's honesty?
> A: Yes, sir.
> Q: That's all.

Now the game has certainly changed. The rape allegation
is now fully revealed and the prosecution is forced to deal
with it. But how? There are three ways to steer into this
skid. One way is to agree that Mrs. Manion was raped,
but argue that Lt. Manion was in control of his faculties.
A second way is to skirt the issue of whether the rape actually happened, but claim that Lt. Manion didn't believe
the rape actually happened and was in control of his faculties. The third option is to claim that Mrs. Manion is lying
and instead had a consensual encounter with Mr. Quill
and that Lt. Manion killed Mr. Quill while in control of
his faculties. Let's see what they choose.

Mr. Lodwick redirects:

> Q: Just a moment. Sergeant Dirgo, did you look for
> the panties elsewhere than the lane in the woods?
> A: We looked in Barney Quill's car, and his room at
> the hotel. We didn't find the panties.

Q: Do you know why Mrs. Manion requested a lie detector test?

A: I know what she said.

Q: What was that?

A: She said she wanted everybody to believe her story, because she knew it would help her husband.

Q: Was that the only reason she gave?

A: She said she'd already sworn to her husband; she wanted everybody else to believe her too.

Q: Did Mrs. Manion say how she'd sworn to her husband?

A: Yes, sir, she said she'd sworn on a rosary.

Q: Sergeant, this lane in the woods, what's it used for? Where does it go?

A: It used to be a logging road. It doesn't go anyplace. It just stops.

Q: Who uses it now?

A: It's a road kids drive down to park.

Q: You mean, it's a lover's lane?

A: I think so, yes, sir.

Q: The witness is yours, Mr. Biegler.

The case within the case is now fully revealed. Finally able to argue that the defendant lost control of his faculties because of his wife's rape, Mr. Biegler must deal with an opponent who now directly refutes the defense theory and offers an alternative explanation: Mrs. Manion was engaged in a consensual encounter with Mr. Quill and is lying about being raped.

Dr. Dompierree

The prosecution's sixth witness is Doctor Dompierree, and he is examined by Claude Dancer:

> Q: Doctor Dompierree, did you have occasion to come to the county jail on the night of August the 15th of this year?
> A: I did.
> Q: Who called you to the jail?
> A: The police authorities.
> Q: What did they want you to do?
> A: They wanted me to make a test for the presence of sperm on the person of a Mrs. Frederick Manion. I made the test.
> Q: In making this test, what was your conclusion?
> A: Negative, there was none.

Mr. Biegler cross-examines for the defense:

> Q: Doctor, in making these tests, did you notice any bruises or marks on Mrs. Manion at that time?
> A: I did.
> Q: Were you asked to determine the reasons for these bruises?
> A: I was not.

These are excellent questions and the best place for Mr. Biegler to go. Perhaps the best pieces of evidence that Mrs. Manion was raped are the bruises and marks on her person. But Mr. Biegler would do better if he had dug deeper and asked more questions about the size, placement, and

212 The Absolute Beginner's Guide to Cross-Examination

type of bruises/marks she had (like he should have with the previous witness). The details would have kept the scene before the jury and made it harder for the prosecution to argue that they were all caused by the defendant.

Q: Where did you do the laboratory work in your test for sperm?

A: St. Margaret's Hospital in this city.

Q: Who worked up the slides for you?

A: Technicians at the hospital.

Q: Well, wouldn't it have been better to have the slides worked up by a pathologist or an expert in this field?

A: Yes, but the police were in a hurry, and I happened to know that this young fellow came on at seven in the morning.

Q: Wouldn't it have been especially better to wait for the expert if the possible question of rape hung on the result?

A: It would have been.

This line of questioning is misguided. Mr. Biegler does not have any basis to argue that the conclusion is erroneous due to a technical error. This is the same kind of spaghetti against the wall tactic we saw during his examination of Mr. Parquette.

Q: Now, doctor, in the newspaper on the evening of August the 16th it was stated that you found no evidence of rape. Is that true?

A: It is not true. I made no such statement.

Q: But did you form an opinion as to whether Mrs. Manion had been raped?

A: No.

Q: Why didn't you form an opinion?

A: It's impossible to tell if a mature, married woman has been raped.

Mr. Biegler has stopped too soon. It is unfortunate since his previous cross-examination of Dr. Raschid (the prosecution's first witness) about the absence of sperm's significance now looks prescient. Let us recall what was asked and answered on this topic:

Q: Now, doctor, if a woman says she's had intercourse with a certain man and this man is proved fertile, yet no evidence is found in the woman's body, couldn't a lawyer—say a prosecuting attorney—use this as evidence that the woman is lying?

A: Yes, prosecution could use that, though certainly it would not be conclusive that she was lying.

Q: Why not?

A: Well, there could be several reasons why the test on her was negative. The use of a contraceptive or possibly there was no completion on the part of the man.

There it is, already done for Mr. Biegler, by Mr. Biegler. In the end, the prosecution called this witness for a purpose that was not provable and the defense did not make them fully pay for it.

Claude Dancer re-directs for the prosecution:

Q: Doctor, did you have an opinion about whether or not she'd had any recent relations with a man?
A: In so far as no sperm was present, it didn't appear that she had had recent relations with a man.

Mr. Biegler re-crosses for the defense:

Q: Just one more question, doctor. The fact that no evidence was present in her body does not mean that she was not raped, does it?
A: No.
Q: Do you know what constitutes rape under the law?
A: Yes, sir. Violation is sufficient for rape. There need not be a completion.

Mr. Biegler again misses the point he previously made with Dr. Raschid: that no sperm could be present due to the use of a contraceptive or if there had not been completion. Finally, don't say "just one more question" since you will never know for sure that it will be true.

Alphonse Paquette

The prosecution then re-called Alphonse Paquette, and he was examined by Claude Dancer:

Q: The people recall Alphonse Paquette to the stand. Your Honor, since counsel for the defense has forced the question of rape, it becomes necessary to take this additional testimony from Mr. Paquette.

J: You're still under oath, Mr. Paquette

Q: Mr. Paquette, would you take a look at Mrs. Manion seated there behind the defense table? Was she dressed in this manner on the night of the shooting?

A: No.

Q: How was she dressed?

A: She had on a real tight skirt and sweater kind of thing, sort of glued on. She was wearing a pair of red shoes with high heels.

Q: Was she wearing hose?

A: No, she was bare-legged.

Q: Was she wearing a hat?

A: No.

Q: Mr. Paquette, what kind of hair does Mrs. Manion have under that hat?

Q: [Biegler] Well, we'd be very happy to show the court Mrs. Manion's hair. Mrs. Manion, would you take off your hat please?

Mr. Biegler's "offer" to have Mrs. Manion remove her hat was anything but an act of sportsmanship. Instead, Mr. Biegler understood that Mr. Dancer's question was attacking the defense's credibility and arguing that Mrs. Manion was now trying to downplay her looks. Mr. Biegler instead tries to protect credibility and appear that they have nothing to hide.

Q: Thank you, Mr. Biegler. Mr. Paquette, was she wearing glasses that night?

A: I think she was when she played pinball.

Q: Considering the tight skirt and the tight sweater and the bare legs, what was the result in her appearance?

A: Well . . .

Q: Would you say Mrs. Manion was deliberately enticing and voluptuous?

Q: [Biegler] Your Honor, the defense will concede that Mrs. Manion, when dressed informally, Mrs. Manion is an astonishingly beautiful woman. Well, Mrs. Manion, stand up please, as a matter of fact—take off your glasses—as a matter of fact, it's pretty easy to understand why her husband became temporarily deranged when he saw such beauty bruised and torn by a beast.

Q: Your Honor, I protest. Mr. Biegler is perhaps the least disciplined and most completely out of order attorney I have ever seen in a courtroom.

J: The jury will ignore Mr. Biegler's oration.

Mr. Biegler clearly understands the importance of credibility and has again tried to appear willing to disclose anything to the trier of fact. And for good measure, he then takes this a step further and marries it into an inappropriate argument to the jury advancing his theory of defense.

Q: Was Mrs. Manion drinking heavily that night?

A: I sold her six drinks myself, and then Barney came over and got some more for her. I don't remember how many.

Q: Would you say that she was tight?

A: Oh, she was high, all right.

Q: What did she do to make you think she was high?

A: Well, she took off her shoes and went barefooted, and when she played pinball she'd kind of swish around to give the machine English.

Q: You mean, she was flipping her hips around?

A: Yeah.

Q: Anything else?

A: When she made a good score, she jumped up and down and squealed like women do.

Q: She was playing pinball with Barney Quill that night, wasn't she?

A: Yes, sir.

Q: What was her attitude towards Barney Quill?

A: Friendly, I guess you could call it.

Q: More than friendly, would you say?

A: I thought so.

Q: Why did you think so?

A: She'd kind of lean on him, and a couple of times she bumped him with her hip.

Q: Would you say that Mrs. Manion was making a play for Barney Quill?

Q: [Biegler] Objection. That calls for an assumption on the part of the witness, your Honor.

I would argue that this objection was a mistake by Mr. Biegler because everyone has already heard the answer in their minds and understands that is the witness's position. As such, this needs to be dealt with since it is now unavoidable.

Q: I withdraw the question. Would you say that Mrs. Manion was free and easy with Barney Quill?

A: I would.

Mr. Biegler cross-examines for the defense:

Q: Mr. Paquette, the attorney for the People asked you if Mrs. Manion was tight, and you said that she was high. Now, speaking as a bartender, what's the distinction between the two?

A: I don't think I understand.

Time to Pull the Chain.

Q: Well, I mean, when we say that a person's tight, we usually mean that they're a little stupid with drink, isn't that so?

A: I guess that's about it, yes.

Q: And if they're high they're gay and enjoying themselves?

A: Yes.

This was not Pulling the Chain. Mr. Biegler should have, but did not make the witness pay for his evasion. The witness is playing the same game from his original cross-examination where he understood the prosecution's question, but can't understand the same thing when Mr. Biegler asks it. And that is what this cross-examination should now turn into, an exposé of his evasiveness. For example:

Q: *Mr. Parquette, you were asked on direct examination if Mrs. Manion was tight and you said she was high?*

A: *Yes.*

Q: *You understood the difference between being tight and high when Mr. Dancer asked you the question and now you claim not to understand the difference when I ask you?*

These are the kind of credibility damaging gifts that cross-examiners cannot miss opening up. The next thing to do is deal head-on with this witness's claim that Mrs. Manion was making a play for Mr. Quill.

Q: *Mr. Paquette, your claim that Mrs. Manion was making a play for Mr. Quill that evening is only based on your observations, correct?*

A: *Yes, that's the way it looked to me.*

Q: *And the basis of those observations of Mrs. Manion were that she was happy, that she was drinking in a tavern, she was playing pinball without shoes on, that she would get excited when she was doing well at pinball, and because she was acting friendly toward the owner of the tavern?*

A: *Yes.*

The name of the game is to establish that the witness's basis for his assertion is without merit. It is easier to knock a witness's opinion down when they put themselves into an over-extended position. Thus, Mr. Biegler should not be afraid of the witness's opinion, but should use it and the facts as a weapon against him.

Mr. Biegler continues:

Q: In other words, Mrs. Manion was happy. Well, now, is there anything wrong with being happy in Thunder Bay Inn?

A: No.

Q: Thunder Bay itself is a resort, isn't it? Swimming, fishing, that sort of thing?

A: Yes.

Q: Is there anything unusual about seeing a barefooted woman in Thunder Bay?

A: No.

Q: So Mrs. Manion's taking her shoes off in Thunder Bay doesn't necessarily mean that she was being unladylike, does it?

A: I guess not.

Q: Yes or no?

A. No.

Now Mr. Biegler is getting with the program of attacking the witness's hollow claim. Then, a well-executed Pull of the Chain using the ask-it-again technique. Not only did Mr. Biegler get the answer he wanted, but the witness's credibility suffered as a result of the evasion. A two-for-one special.

Q: Now you testified that Mrs. Manion was squealing and jumping up and down. And swishing—I think that was the expression you used—swishing her hips around the pinball machine. Now was she creating a disturbance, was she attracting a crowd?

A: No.

Q: Were all the men at the bar, were they all standing around watching Mrs. Manion?

A: No.

Q: But you were very conscious of Mrs. Manion. You were conscious enough so that you could tell us all about her actions.

A: Yes.

Q: And certainly Barney Quill, he was conscious of Mrs. Manion, because he was playing pinball with Mrs. Manion, wouldn't you say so?

A: Yes.

Q: So it seems that only you and Barney Quill were acutely aware of Mrs. Manion and her actions and her appearance; maybe good old Barney, when he came up to get a couple of drinks from you, maybe he winked and said, "Alphonse, I'm going to take this babe out and rape her" and maybe you said, "Do it once for me, boss!"

Q: [Prosecution] Objection! Objection!

Q: No more questions!

Mr. Biegler was effectively steering into the skid by using the direct examination points to make the alternative argument that there was nothing wrong with Mrs. Manion's behavior. However, Mr. Biegler's last question (which was not a question) could have ended with him being held in contempt of court.

The main problem with Mr. Biegler's last statement is that he does not put the argument into the form of a question because he knows that the witness will disagree with him. But that is not what matters. What matters is whether the mosaic is convincing enough that the trier of fact hears your answer in their minds. If they don't, then the question is not worth asking. Here, Mr. Biegler simply doesn't have evidence or support under the Rule of Probability to make an effective argument that Mr. Parquette knew that Mr. Quill was going to rape Mrs. Manion or that he encouraged it.

This witness was recalled by the prosecution to make the argument that Mrs. Manion's behavior indicated that she had engaged in a consensual encounter with Mr. Quill. This general line of questioning and many of the specific questions might well not be permitted in a modern courtroom depending on the circumstances. However, we are taking it as it happened so figuring out how to deal with it is the object. Thus, the attainable goal of this cross-examination is to use the Hitchhiking and Limiting techniques to demonstrate that Mrs. Manion's behavior did not demonstrate her desire to engage in a consensual relationship with Mr. Quill instead of trying to make this witness a co-conspirator.

Lt. Frederick Manion

The defense's first witness was the defendant, Lieutenant Frederick Manion, who testified on direct examination:

Q: All right, now let's get at this rosary thing. Now, it has been testified that your wife swore to you on a rosary that she'd been raped by Barney Quill. Now, did you ask your wife to swear on a rosary?

A: My wife was hysterical; she wasn't making much sense. I thought that if I asked her to swear an oath on a rosary, it might serve to calm her, make her think more clearly.

Q: Did the rosary help?

A: She was able to tell me in detail what had happened.

Mr. Biegler knows the swearing on the rosary is a problem and is trying to build a protective theory for the inevitable cross-examination on this subject.

Q: All right, go on from there. What did you do then, lieutenant?

A: Well I had her lie on the bed, and I got some cold cloths for her head. And, oh yes, I gave her a drink of brandy. After a while, she became calm, and seemed to go to sleep. And I went to the closet. I got my gun, and I loaded it.

Q: Was it in your mind to kill Barney Quill?

A: No.

Q: Well, then why'd you go to your closet, and get your gun and load it?

A: Well, I knew I had to go to Quill's place; I thought I might need it.

Q: Why?

A: I knew Mr. Quill kept guns behind the bar. I was afraid he might shoot me.

Q: Might shoot you if you did what? What were you going to do?

A: I'm not sure. I remember having some idea of finding him and holding him while I called the police.

Q: Well, that, that, Mr. What's his name, Mr. Lemon right at the tourist court there; he was a deputy sheriff, why didn't you get him to go with you?

A: He just seemed to be the old caretaker of the park. Maybe because I wasn't thinking about anything too clearly excepting finding Barney Quill.

Q: Why didn't you go to a telephone, call the State Police before you went to the bar?

A: I don't know. I was in sort of a daze. It was a horrible thing to see what had been done to my wife.

Q: Now, you say that you were in sort of a daze. When you got to the bar, did you see that the bar was crowded?

A: I didn't see anybody at the bar except Barney Quill. He was the only person I saw.

Q: What was he doing?

A: I think he was just standing there behind the bar.

Q: Did he make a threatening move to get a gun?

A: I don't know. He may have. I don't know.

Q: All right. Now, you say you went there to find him, hold him. Why did you shoot him?

A: I don't remember shooting him.

Q: Now when you left the bar, do you remember Alphonse Paquette coming up to you and stopping you and saying, "You better not run away from this," and your reply, "Do you want some too, buster?" Remember that?

A: I seem to have a vague recollection of somebody speaking to me, but I don't remember what I said or what was said to me.

As you will recall, there were no available tools to deal with this statement by Mr. Paquette on his cross-examination. Instead of going after the previous witness empty handed, this is the time for the defense to deal with it by claiming no memory of it (which is probably the only thing they could say). The point is that problems need to be dealt with, but it is not always possible to do it exactly when you want to.

Q: When did you realize that you'd shot Quill?

A: I was getting a drink of water; I remember my throat was so dry it hurt. When I put the glass down, I saw the gun on the kitchen sink beside the tap. I noticed the gun was empty.

Q: Now, I'd like you to show the court and jury just how you knew this gun was empty.

A: Well, this gadget here, when it sticks up, you know the last round's been fired.

Q: Lieutenant Manion, on the night of the shooting, did you love your wife?

A: Yes, sir.

Q: Do you still love her?

A: Very much.

Claude Dancer cross-examines for the People:

Q: How many men have you killed?

Q: [Biegler] Now wait a minute, your Honor. A man's war record, in Lieutenant Manion's case, a great one, certainly shouldn't be used against him.

Q: Your Honor, I'm as patriotic as the next man, but the simple truth is war can condition a man to killing other men. I simply want to determine how conditioned the lieutenant may be to the use of firearms on other human beings.

J: I don't quite like the question, Mr. Biegler, but I don't see how I can exclude it. Let him answer.

A: I know I killed at least four men in Korea, three with a hand grenade, and one with my service automatic. I may have killed others. A soldier doesn't always know.

Q: Now, lieutenant, in these acts of killing, did you ever have a lapse of memory such as you had when you killed Barney Quill?

A: No, sir.

Mr. Dancer immediately challenges the argument that the defendant lost control of his faculties by juxtaposing it against the other times the defendant has killed someone. While the issue of whether Mrs. Manion was raped or engaged in a consensual encounter has taken center stage, the material issue remains whether or not the defendant lost control of his faculties.

Q: Did you ever have a lapse of memory during battle?

A: No, sir.

Q: Were you ever submitted to a constant barrage, constantly in a sweat for many hours, constantly under attack or attacking?

A: Many times.

Q: Were you ever treated for shellshock, battle fatigue, or any war neuroses or psychoses?

A: No, sir.

Q: Did you ever experience any unusual mental state during the war?

A: I do remember having one great urge.

Q: What was that?

A: To get the hell out and go home.

A brilliant controlled open-ended question where no answer could hurt him and where the witness could (and did) hurt himself.

J: You would do well to consider the seriousness of the situation you are in.

A: I'm sorry, your Honor.

Q: I sympathize with the lieutenant. I suspect he has the same feeling about getting out of jail. But the main point here, lieutenant, is that at no time during your war service did you have a record of mental disturbance. You were always in complete possession of your faculties?

A: Yes, sir, that's right.

Mr. Dancer has done a fine job of using controlled open-ended questions to control the witness and establish that he has never, even while in combat, suffered from the type of condition he now claims. Mr. Dancer heard the witness, created an expert trap, and then made him pay for his glib answer by using it as an argument that the defendant is trying to escape justice.

Reasonable people can differ about whether this was or was not a wise line of questioning. On the one hand, it serves the prosecution's argument that Lt. Manion has none of the predicate history indicating the loss of control here. On the other hand, the defense could well argue that being in combat is materially different than hearing that your wife has been raped. Weighing those issues, along with the probability that it makes the defendant look like a war hero, it is not a very enticing line of inquiry, especially compared to the more important ones that were not dealt with.

For example, Mr. Dancer does not attack the issues of the rosary or Lt. Manion's reasons for going to the bar if not to kill Mr. Quill. If the prosecution's theory is that Lt. Manion did not believe that his wife was raped or that she had engaged in a consensual encounter with Mr. Quill, then these issues need to be challenged. Moreover, the defense knows that these are problems and expects them to be challenged, which is why they have built their defensive walls around these issues on direct examination. Here's an example of additional areas for cross-examination by the prosecution:

Q: *You claimed on direct examination that you wanted your wife to swear about what happened on a rosary because she wasn't making sense and that you thought this would calm her down?*

A: *Yes. She calmed down after she swore on the rosary and made more sense.*

Q: *You asked your wife to swear to the truthfulness of the story on one of the most important symbols of the Catholic faith because you wanted her to calm down?*

A: *Yes.*

Q: *No, Lt. Manion. You demanded your wife swear an oath of truth on a rosary because you didn't believe her story about being raped by Mr. Quill, didn't you?*

A: *That's not true.*

Q: *You didn't believe that she had been raped by him and instead thought that she was cheating on you?*

A: *That's not true.*

Q: *You caught her coming back into the house after being with Mr. Quill and you hit her, didn't you?*

A: *I only hit her to try and calm her down. I didn't cause those bruises; Mr. Quill did.*

Q: *You hit her in a jealous rage, just like you had done before?*

A: *That's not what happened.*

Q: *You have hit your wife in a jealous rage before, haven't you?*

A: *Yes.*

Q: *And you previously attacked another man in a jealous rage for merely cutting in on the dance floor, didn't you?*

A: *Yes.*

Q: *You hit your wife for being with Mr. Quill and then you decided to grab your gun and go after Mr. Quill for being with her?*

A: *That's not what happened.*

Q: *You claim that Mr. Quill raped your wife, but you didn't call the police?*

A: *I wasn't thinking clearly.*

Q: *You were thinking clearly enough that you made your wife swear on a rosary, had her lie on the bed, got her some cold cloths for her head, gave her a drink of brandy, went to the closet, got your gun, and loaded every bullet into it?*

A: *Yes.*

Q: *You were thinking clearly enough that you decided to grab your loaded gun because Mr. Quill had a gun at the bar?*

A: *Yes.*

Q: *You were thinking clearly enough to do all of those things, but you claim that you were only going to the bar to hold Mr. Quill for the police when you could have easily called them instead?*

A: *I wasn't thinking clearly about that.*

Q: *You decided not to call the police because you were jealous that Mr. Quill was with your wife and after you hit her, you decided to kill him for it, didn't you?*

A: *No, that's not what happened.*

I am confident that this area must be attacked to make the full argument that the defendant did not lose control of his faculties. The key is to decide on the theory of the case and to propound that theory through the substance of the questions. The defendant's answers are not what matters, only whether the substance of the questions persuades the trier of fact to agree with *your* answers.

Laura Manion

The defense's second witness was Laura Manion, who testified on direct examination:

Q: Now how long after you told your husband what
   had happened did he leave the trailer?
A: I don't know exactly. Everything was kind of fuzzy.
   I was faint, and I lay down on the bed. He sat
   beside me. I vaguely remember his getting up and
   going out. I remember wondering if he was going
   for a doctor, and then he came back in. It seemed
   like just a few seconds, but it must have been longer. I must have gone to sleep. When he came back
   in, he sat on the bed and he had a gun in his hand
   and I said, "What are you going to do?" and he
   said, "I think I've already done it. I think I've killed
   Barney Quill."
Q: Are you sure he didn't say, "I killed Barney Quill"?
A: No, I remember distinctly. "I think I killed Barney
   Quill."
Q: Then what did you do?
A: I put my arms around him and began to cry, and
   I said, "You'd better go to Mr. Lemon." And my
   husband said, "I'd forgot about that."
Q: Now, what did he mean? Forgot about what?
A: Well, he meant that he'd forgotten that Mr. Lemon
   was a deputy sheriff, and he said, "Yes, I'll go turn
   myself in to Mr. Lemon."
Q: Yes, I see. Your Honor, I have no other direct ques-
   tions at this time. But since I'm sure it's difficult to

visualize the part a little dog played on this night, I should like a few minutes to show the court this remarkable little animal.

J: Any objections?

Q: [Dancer] I'm sure if we raise an objection, your Honor, Mr. Biegler will declare that we are haters of all small furry animals.

J: A creature that cannot talk will be a welcome relief. Bring in the dog.

Q: Will the deputy bring in the dog, please? You can put him right there. C'mon, c'mon, c'mon, c'mon, c'mon, c'mon. That's a boy. Now, I'll ask Mrs. Manion to bring a flashlight for the dog. Now I'll ask the court to notice that the dog turned on the light. Well it's easy to see that the mutt doesn't know who his enemies are.[†]

J: That's enough. Remove the dog please. Witness will resume the stand.

Claude Dancer cross-examines for the government:

Q: Mrs. Manion, may I congratulate you on your well-trained pet? May I also say that I'm pleased to see you're not today hiding your lovely hair under a hat?

Q: [Biegler] Your Honor, is the assistant attorney general from Lansing pitching woo, or is he going to cross-examine?

J: Let's get on with it.

---

† In the film, Mrs. Manion brings the flashlight to the dog, which then turns it on with its paw. The dog then carries the flashlight in its mouth and jumps onto the lap of Mr. Dancer.

This statement is intended to argue that Mrs. Manion has been intentionally minimizing her attractiveness during the trial because she thinks it hurts her husband's defense. The statement is totally improper, but what is particularly interesting is Mr. Biegler's response. Instead of making an objection and narration about why it was improper (which is what Mr. Dancer wants so the jury can hear it), he instead wisely steers into the skid and pretends that the comment is about something else entirely. Just because we can object doesn't mean we should. Masterful.

> Q: What was your occupation before you were married?
> A: Housewife.
> Q: Oh, then you've been married before?
> A: Yes, once.
> Q: I suppose your first husband died?
> A: No.

A devastating controlled open-ended question. Mr. Dancer knows that Mrs. Manion is not a widow, but makes her say it.

> Q: Did you divorce your first husband to marry Lieutenant Manion?
> Q: [Biegler] Your Honor, if counsel wants to know the grounds for Mrs. Manion's divorce, then let him ask that question.

Mr. Biegler knows where this is going and he is wise not to try and stop it because he cannot. Instead, he tries to steer

234 The Absolute Beginner's Guide to Cross-Examination

into the skid by demanding the prosecution be sharper in its question to make the trier of fact think that the defense welcomes this inquiry.

> Q: What were the grounds for divorce, Mrs. Manion?
> A: Mental cruelty.
> Q: Naturally. And how long after your divorce was it that you married Lieutenant Manion?
> A: I'm not sure.
> Q: [Biegler] May I refresh the witness's memory for Mr. Dancer?
> J: By all means.
> Q: [Biegler] I believe she told me they were married three days after the divorce.
> Q: Thank you, Mr. Biegler. Is that correct, Mrs. Manion?
> A: Yes.

Mrs. Manion unwisely chose an evasive answer because she knows that the truthful answer supports the prosecution's theory of the case. Mr. Biegler sees this and tries to come to her rescue, pretending that they don't mind sharing this at all.

> Q: Then unless yours was a whirlwind courtship, you must have known Lieutenant Manion before your divorce? Did you?
> A: Yes.

The point of this is a propensity argument that Mrs. Manion cheated on her previous husband with Lt. Manion, which would support the argument that Mrs. Manion was cheating on Lt. Manion with Mr. Quill. Mr. Dancer, however, doesn't go all the way in making this point since he only asks whether they knew each other before the divorce. Again, this may well be impermissible in a modern courtroom, but it was permitted here so we deal with it as such. Thus, if you're trying to make a point, you should make it all the way.

> Q: Mrs. Manion, what is your religious affiliation?
> A: I'm a Catholic.
> Q: Catholic in good standing?
> A: Well, no, the divorce, you know.
> Q: You mean you were excommunicated because of the divorce and the remarriage?
> A: Yes.
> Q: Mrs. Manion, wouldn't you say that a Catholic who can blithely ignore one of the cardinal rules of her church, could also easily ignore an oath taken on one of its artifacts? Say, an oath taken on a rosary?
> A: I don't think that's true.
> Q: Wouldn't you think that there would be some doubt about the integrity of such a person?
> A: I don't know. All I know is that the rosary means something to me.

This line of questioning juxtaposing the breaking of the marriage vows and the swearing on the rosary is not well executed. The central problem is the formation of the questions asking her "wouldn't you say" and "wouldn't

236 The Absolute Beginner's Guide to Cross-Examination

you think." These expressions give the witness the opportunity to explain her values and how these two colliding principles can live together.

Instead, these questions are more effective when clearly stating the argument for the tier of fact: "Your sworn marriage vows, taken in a church before god, were more significant than your swearing on a church artifact after being excommunicated from the church for breaking your marriage oath, weren't they?"

> Q: I see. Well, I'll pass on to something else. Mrs. Manion, you testified that your husband came home late from his work on the night of the shooting. Were you a little angry about his being late?
>
> A: I guess I was a little put out.
>
> Q: Did you have an argument?
>
> A: Not much. A little.
>
> Q: When you left the trailer to go to the inn, did your husband know you were going?
>
> A: He was asleep.
>
> Q: Was part of your reason for going without his knowledge because you were vexed?
>
> A: Well, I'd been ironing all day, and I—Yes, I guess that's true.
>
> Q: Would you have gone to the inn if your husband had been awake?
>
> A: He probably would have gone with me.
>
> Q: But would you have gone alone?
>
> A: Not if he didn't want me to.
>
> Q: Would he have not wanted you to?
>
> A: I'm not sure. I don't know how to answer that.

The last three questions were poorly constructed. Mr. Dancer previously got a very important answer that she had gone out without her husband's knowledge and that she was mad at him. He would be better served to lean on those given his theory of the case.

> Q: Have you ever gone to the Thunder Bay Inn or elsewhere in Thunder Bay alone at night?
> A: Yes, sometimes.
> Q: Did your husband know you were going?
> A: Not always. He goes to sleep early and sometimes I'm restless.
> Q: Where did you go on these occasions?
> A: Oh, I'd take a walk by the lake or went to the bingo place, maybe to the Inn.
> Q: Ever go to meet another man?
> A: No I didn't; I never did that.
> Q: You mean to say, Mrs. Manion, a lovely woman like yourself, attracted to men, lonely, restless, that you never once—
> Q: [Biegler] Objection, your Honor. Witness has answered the question about other men. Counsel is now making a veiled suggestion to the jury.
> Q: I withdraw the question. Now, Mrs. Manion, on these occasional excursions into the night, did you always go and return home alone?
> A: Of course.

If Mr. Biegler is going to object to the first question, then he should have objected to this one, as well, since it goes to the same point. In for a penny, in for a pound.

Q: Mrs. Manion, you testified that the reason you got into Barney Quill's car was because you were afraid to go home alone. Why were you so frightened on this particular night?

A: I said that it was because he told me bears had been seen around.

Q: Was this the first time you'd heard that bears came around Thunder Bay to pick up scraps?

A: No.

Q: Had you seen the bears before?

A: Yes.

Q: Oh, this was just the first time you were afraid of them?

A: No, I was always afraid of them.

Q: Oh, this was just the first time you were not afraid to allow a man to take you home from one of your evening prowls?

Q: [Biegler] Objection. Use of the word prowls meant to mislead the jury.

J: Sustained.

Q: I apologize, Mrs. Manion. I didn't mean to imply that you were a huntress. Was this the first time that you were not afraid to allow a man to take you home from one of your evening walks?

A: Well, it wasn't just that, it was—

Q: Oh, come now, Mrs. Manion, you should be able to answer that straight off. That's a simple enough question.

It is almost never a good idea to cut off a witness, especially when they are floundering under a difficult question.

Mr. Dancer thinks he is scoring a point by demonstrating that Mrs. Manion is unable to give a quick and succinct answer, but this is a mistake. If a witness is taking too long to answer and their answer is unfocused, then the trier of fact will come to that credibility determination on their own. Instead of letting the witness hurt themselves, cutting them off instead provides them a lifeline.

> Q: [Biegler] Your Honor, how can the witness answer straight off if the counsel keeps interrupting the answer?
>
> J: The witness seemed a little slow to me, Mr. Biegler. However, let her complete her answers before you interrupt.
>
> Q: Of course, your Honor. In any case, Mr. Biegler's objection has given Mrs. Manion sufficient time to think of an answer to my question. You've thought of one, haven't you, Mrs. Manion?
>
> A: What I was going to say was, I didn't want to offend Mr. Quill by making him think that I was afraid of him or didn't like him. He'd been very pleasant to my husband and me when we'd been in his bar.
>
> Q: That's very good, Mrs. Manion, very good indeed.

Mr. Dancer interrupts the witness, the defense objects, the judge rules, and the witness has plenty of time to think of an answer. Mr. Dancer knows this and makes an inappropriate comment about it, but he has only himself to blame for cutting her off.

And if that weren't bad enough, Mr. Dancer also doesn't hear Mrs. Manion's answer, which doesn't actually answer the question he asked.

Mr. Dancer asked "[w]as this the first time that you were not afraid to allow a man to take you home from one of your evening walks?" And Mrs. Manion's answer instead gave a different reason why she got in the car with Mr. Quill that night from the one she previously gave of being concerned about bears. Mr. Dancer has missed an opportunity to Pull the Chain on the witness for both not answering his question and for shifting her explanation about getting into the car with Mr. Quill.

Q: [Biegler] Your Honor, please.
J: The attorney for the People will reserve his comments for the arguments.
Q: I will ask you this question, Mrs. Manion. Was this the first time you had been in Barney Quill's car at night?
J: Mrs. Manion, did you hear the question?

Mr. Dancer appears to have learned his lesson and lets the witness ponder the question in uncomfortable silence to the point where the judge feels compelled to interject.

A: Yes, I heard. Yes, it was the first time.
Q: Would you raise your voice a little, Mrs. Manion?
A: I said it was the first time.

Remember, it is not just the answer that the witness gives that matters, but also how she presents the answer. Now we only have the cold transcript here, but it is reasonable to assume based on how she answered that the trier of fact either believed that Mrs. Manion's answer was not credible or that she was shaken by such an allegation. The result is an open question where a crisp answer would have been the end of it.

> Q: Now, Mrs. Manion, I'm quite concerned about the lost panties. Would you describe this article of clothing to the court, please?
> A: They were nylon and had lace up the sides and there was a label in them of the place I got them. The Smart Shop in Phoenix, Arizona.
> Q: What was the color of the panties?
> A: I believe white.
> Q: You believe?
> A: I have white and pink. They may have been pink.
> Q: You're not sure. Haven't you checked your lingerie to see which pair of panties is missing?
> A: No.

Another missed opportunity to further argue the theory of the case through the substance of the question: "You claim that Mr. Quill raped you, yet you didn't even check to see what color panties were missing in order to tell the police?"

> Q: When your husband came home late for work and you had this little spat, were you already dressed to go out?
> A: No.

Q: When did you dress?

A: After dinner when he was asleep.

Q: It's been stated here that you were bare-legged in the bar. Is that true?

A: Yes.

Q: In your anger at your husband and your haste to get out of the trailer, perhaps you didn't put on any panties either.

Q: [Biegler] Objection. Witness has already testified as to what she was wearing.

J: Sustained.

Q: You always wear panties, Mrs. Manion?

Q: [Biegler] Now, your Honor, I object to this line of questioning. It's immaterial what Ms. Manion does all the time. On the night she was attacked she was wearing panties, and that's all we're concerned about.

Q: Your Honor, Mrs. Manion seems a little bit uncertain about what kind of panties she was wearing and since these panties have not been found, I submit that it's possible she wasn't wearing any and has forgotten about it, that's all I'm trying to get at.

J: You may answer, Mrs. Manion.

Q: Do you always wear panties?

A: No.

Q: On what occasions don't you wear them? When you go out alone at night?

Q: [Biegler] Oh no, no, objection. He says he's going after one thing, and then he goes after another.

J: I'll sustain the objection. Strike out the last two questions and Mrs. Manion's answers. Now, Mr.

Dancer, get off the panties. You've done enough damage.

Q: Yes, your Honor. Mrs. Manion, is your husband a jealous man?

A: He loves me.

Time to Pull the Chain . . .

Q: I'm sure of that, but is your husband excessively jealous?

Q: [Biegler] Your Honor, how can the witness answer that question? What's the norm of jealousy?

J: Can you put your question a little differently, Mr. Dancer?

Sometimes when we object to the form of a question, we only make things worse.

Q: Has your husband ever struck you in a jealous rage?

Q: [Biegler] Your Honor, I think Mr. Dancer is fishing now. What's the relevancy of this question?

Q: Your Honor, the shoe is squeezing Mr. Biegler's foot. In his own words, this is not a high school debate; this a cross-examination in a murder trial.

J: Proceed, Mr. Dancer.

Q: Mrs. Manion, did you ever go out socially in Thunder Bay?

A: Yes, a few times.

Mr. Dancer is going to get there, but I would go back to the same question that was asked before the objection concerning whether Lt. Manion ever hit her in a jealous rage since no answer was given.

Q: When your husband's outfit moved to Thunder Bay, didn't Barney Quill throw a cocktail party for the officers and their wives?

A: Yes.

Q: Didn't your husband strike a young second lieutenant at this party?

A: There was a little scuffle. It wasn't much.

Q: What was it about?

A: I'm not sure I remember.

Q: Were you too drunk to remember?

A: No, I was not. I think it was because the lieutenant was cutting in too much when I was dancing with my husband.

Q: And shortly afterwards, on the veranda of the Inn, didn't your husband slap you hard enough so that you fell against the wall?

A: Well, he was drinking.

Another opportunity to Pull the Chain and ask the same question again until she answers it.

Q: Wasn't this a jealous rage?

A: I don't know.

Another opportunity to Pull the Chain: "Mrs. Manion, your husband attacked the young lieutenant and then slapped you so hard that you fell against a wall for merely cutting in on the dance floor. This was a jealous rage, wasn't it?"

Mr. Dancer continues:

Q: Do you remember why he struck you?
A: Yes.
Q: Wasn't he enraged at you because he thought that you had encouraged this young lieutenant?
A: He might have thought so.
Q: Mrs. Manion, there are witnesses to this whole affair. I'll ask you again: wasn't this a jealous rage?
A: I guess you could call it that.

Another opportunity to Pull the Chain and make the witness directly answer the question after she has twice tried to avoid directly answering it.

Q: Now I'll ask you. On the night of the shooting, what did you swear? What oath did you take on the rosary?
A: It was about Barney Quill raping me.
Q: Why did you swear on a rosary that he'd raped you?
A: For the reason that my husband said, because I was hysterical.
Q: That was the reason he gave for asking you to swear. What was your reason for swearing?
A: So he'd believe me.
Q: Why shouldn't he believe you?
Q: [Biegler] The reason for the use of the rosary has been established. These questions are immaterial.

J: No, I think I'll take the answer, Mr. Biegler.

Q: I'll ask you again, Mrs. Manion: why shouldn't he believe you?

A: Because I wasn't making much sense.

This line of attack about swearing on the rosary is important, but Mr. Dancer is too quick and doesn't hear the witness's answer. Her testimony that she swore on the rosary because she "wasn't making much sense" is an explanation that doesn't make any sense. When a witness offers an explanation that doesn't match up with the conduct at issue, we need to make that clear for the trier of fact. At the end of the intellectual rainbow, people swear on a rosary so that someone else will believe them, not so that they become coherent.

Q: Did he think you'd lie about a thing like that?

Q: [Biegler] Objection, your Honor; Lieutenant Manion has already testified as to what he thought.

J: Sustained.

Q: Did your husband strike you that night? Did he hit you that night?

A: Why, he may have slapped me, because I was hysterical.

Another opportunity to Pull the Chain regarding the evasiveness of whether or not he hit her. Indeed, the bruises and marks on the witness may be the most compelling evidence that she was raped by Mr. Quill. As such, the prosecution needs to argue through the witness that the bruises and marks were caused by the defendant: "He hit you many times, didn't he?"

Q: And didn't you swear to a lie to keep him from hitting you again?

A: No, no, I didn't. I did not.

Q: And hadn't he already beaten you up at the gate when he caught you coming home from a trip down lover's lane with Barney Quill?

Q: [Biegler] Objection, objection, the witness has already testified that she was beaten by Barney Quill.

Q: No more questions.

Now I recognize that this cross-examination will provoke strong emotions. We nevertheless must remember three things: this took place in the 1950s, this was based on a real case, and that the defense theory put forward the question of whether Mrs. Manion was a victim of rape or whether she was lying to protect her husband's murder of an innocent man.

With that said and with our mission to learn the techniques, we must recognize that this is in many ways a masterful cross-examination. Mr. Dancer is able to maintain complete control over the witness while appearing to be doing a direct examination. It is a piercing series of questions painting an argument that Mrs. Manion lied about being raped and that Lt. Manion instead killed Mr. Quill in an act of jealousy.

Dr. Matthew Smith

The defense's third witness was Dr. Matthew Smith, who testified on direct examination:

Q: Doctor, did you examine Lieutenant Manion?

A: Yes, I did.

Q: And have you formed an opinion as to Frederick Manion's mental and emotional state at the time he killed Barney Quill?

A: I have.

Q: And what is that opinion?

A: He was temporarily insane at the time of the shooting.

Q: At the time of the shooting, do you believe he was able to distinguish between right and wrong?

A: He may or may not have been; it doesn't make too much difference.

Q: Now, doctor, as clearly as you can, will you explain Frederick Manion's temporary insanity?

A: It is known as Dissociative Reaction. A psychic shock which creates an almost overwhelming tension which the person in shock must alleviate. In Lieutenant Manion's case, a soldier, it is only natural that he would turn to action. Only direct simple action against Barney Quill would relieve the unbearable tension. This is not too uncommon; for example, in combat, some of the more remarkable heroics take place in this state of mind.

Q: Is there another name for Dissociative Reaction, one we might be more likely to recognize?

A: Yes, it has been known as irresistible impulse.

Q: Now, doctor, a man in the grip of irresistible impulse, would he be likely to go to his neighbor for advice, or call up the police to come to his aid?

A: Completely incompatible.

Q: Yes, but our man was able to think of going and taking out a gun and loading it before setting out to find Quill?

A: Well, that was his conscious mind working, but if no gun had been available, he would have gone anyway.

Q: How would a man look in the grip of Dissociative Reaction?

A: He might appear to be deadly calm, fiercely deliberate.

Q: Uh-hmm. Would you describe his behavior as being like a mailman, delivering the mail?

A: That's not bad. Like a mailman, he would have a job to do, and he would do it.

Mr. Biegler masterfully uses Mr. Paquette's direct examination description of Lt. Manion's behavior at the time of the shooting to support his expert's conclusion and as a weapon against the prosecution.

Claude Dancer cross-examines for the prosecution:

Q: Doctor, did you find any psychosis in Frederick Manion?

A: I did not.

Q: Any neuroses?

A: I found no history of neuroses.

Q: Any history of delusion?

A: None.

Q: Loss of memory?

A: Not before this instance.

Q: Doctor, you stated that the defendant might or might not have been able to distinguish the difference between right and wrong, but that it wouldn't have made much difference, right, is that what you said?

A: Approximately, yes.

Q: Do you mean that at the time of the shooting he could have known the difference between right and wrong?

A: He might have, yes.

Q: Dr. Smith, if the defendant could have known what he was doing, and could have known that it was wrong, how can you come here and testify that he was legally insane?

A: I'm not saying he was legally insane. I'm saying that in his mental condition, it would not have made any difference whether he knew right from wrong. He would still have shot Quill.

Q: Doctor Smith, are you willing to rest your testimony in this case on this opinion?

A: Yes, I am.

Mr. Dancer's cross-examination was excellent, but with one glaring problem: his boat was aimed in the wrong direction. He thought that a defendant could not sufficiently plead insanity if he could distinguish right from wrong. Thus, he thought this cross-examination sealed the case for his side. However, after the testimony, he learned about *People vs. Durfee*,[‡] a then-controlling precedent from 1886 permitting the irresistible impulse theory where a person could distinguish right from wrong, but nevertheless be compelled beyond their control to commit an act.

This is an excellent example of an able cross-examiner expertly working the wind, but still ending up on the rocks because his boat was aimed in the wrong direction.

Dr. Gregory Harcourt

The prosecution calls their first rebuttal witness, Dr. Gregory Harcourt, who is examined by Claude Dancer:

Q: Dr. Harcourt, where did you receive your university training?

A: Johns Hopkins in Baltimore, Maryland.

Q: And where do you practice now?

A: I'm medical superintendent of the Bonder State Hospital for the Insane.

Q: It's been stated here that Dissociative Reaction or irresistible impulse is not uncommon among soldiers in combat. Do you agree with that statement, Dr. Harcourt?

A: I do, but not as it was put by Dr. Smith.

Q: Where would you depart from Dr. Smith?

A: Well, Dissociative Reaction is not something that comes out of the blue, and disappears as quickly. It can only occur, even among a soldier in combat, if the individual has a psychoneurotic condition of long standing.

---

‡   62 Mich. 487 (1886)

Q: It's been testified here that a psychiatric examination of the defendant showed no evidence of neuroses and no history of Dissociative Reaction. You further heard it testified that the defendant's behavior on the night of the shooting was cool and direct. As an observer, do you remember this testimony?

A: Yes.

Q: From this, have you formed an opinion about the defendant's sanity on the night of the shooting?

A: I am of the opinion that he was in sufficient possession of his faculties, so that he was not dominated by his unconscious mind.

Q: In other words, he was not in the grip of irresistible impulse.

A: In my opinion, he was not.

Biegler cross-examines for the defense:

Q: Dr. Harcourt, psychiatry is an effort to probe into the dark, undiscovered world of the mind, and in there the world might be round, it could be square. Your opinion could be wrong; Dr. Smith's opinion could be right, isn't that true?

A: I'd be a poor doctor if I didn't agree with that, but I believe my opinion to be right.

Mr. Dancer probably wished he thought of this question on his cross-examination of Dr. Smith.

Q: Now do you think you might change your opinion if you would examine the defendant as Dr. Smith did?

A: I don't believe so.

Q: But Dr. Smith's was made under better circumstances, wasn't it?

A: If you mean that he was able to examine the man,
yes.

Q: Yeah. Thank you, doctor.

Mr. Biegler got very lucky with the witness's answers and
even luckier that there was no re-direct. The witness's
opinion on direct examination was that:

A: Well, Dissociative Reaction is not something that
comes out of the blue, and disappears as quickly.
It can only occur, even among a soldier in combat,
if the individual has a psychoneurotic condition of
long standing. [Emphasis added.]

The defendant inarguably does not have a psychoneurotic
condition of long standing. Nevertheless, Mr. Biegler got
the witness to change his opinion based on the irrelevant
issue of the lack of a personal examination. The "I don't
believe so" answer should instead have been:

A: No, *because examining him wouldn't have mattered since Dissociative Reaction can only occur
if the individual had a psychoneurotic condition of
long standing and the defendant doesn't have one.*

We will never know why the witness answered the question the way he did instead of the way he could have.
The most reasonable assumption is that the form of Mr.

254 The Absolute Beginner's Guide to Cross-Examination

Biegler's question put pressure on him to appear less than 100 percent certain since he did not examine the defendant. Whatever the reason, the moral of the story is that things do not always go as they should on the witness stand, especially when we put pressure on the witness.

Dwayne Miller

The prosecution calls their second rebuttal witness, Dwayne Miller, who is examined by Claude Dancer:

> Q: State your name, please.
> A: Dwayne Miller, but most folks call me Duke.
> Q: Where do you presently reside, Mr. Miller?
> A: Across the alley in the jail.
> Q: Do you know the Defendant Frederick Manion?
> A: I got to know him in the past few weeks. His cell's right next to mine.
> Q: When was the last conversation you had with the lieutenant?
> A: Except for hello, this morning.
> Q: Did you discuss his trial last night?
> A: Yeah, some.
> Q: Will you tell the court what Lt. Manion had to say about the trial?
> A: Well, I said, "Thing's looking up, Lieutenant?" And he said, "I've got it made, buster." He said, "I fooled my lawyer, I fooled that head-shrinker, and I'm going to fool that bunch of corncobbers on the jury."
> Q: Mr. Miller, are you certain that Lt. Manion said, "I've got it made, buster?"

A: That's what he said.

Q: Mr. Miller, did Lt. Manion say anything else?

A: When he got out, the first thing he'd do was to kick that bitch from here to kingdom come.

Q: To whom was he referring?

A: To his wife.

Biegler cross-examines for the defense:

Q: What are you in jail for?

A: Arson. I copped out and I'm waiting for a sentence.

Q: And how many other offenses have you committed?

A: Well, I was in reform school when I was a kid, but that's all.

Mr. Biegler wisely goes after the witness's credibility in the beginning since it will help win the credibility fight about whether or not the defendant said those things. Moreover, the prosecutor's failure to elicit this information only makes the Credibility Attack more potent.

Q: Your Honor, I'd like to see this man's criminal record.

J: Do you have his record, Mr. Lodwick?

Q: [Lodwick] Yes, sir. Here it is.

Q: Well, your record here shows that you've been in prison five times for felonies in three different states. Three times for arson, and twice for assault with a deadly weapon.

A: Yeah.

Q: It also shows you've done time for larceny, indecent exposure, window peeping, and disorderly conduct. Is this your true record?

A: Them things are never right.

Mr. Biegler has done well Pulling the Chain on this witness through the impeachment method and he has to pull it hard because this entire case now turns on the witness's credibility. However, the witness's last answer continues to be evasive, and I would not have stopped here.

Q: How did you get the ear of the prosecution in order to tell them about this conversation you had with Lt. Manion?

A: The DA was taking us to his office.

Q: Taking who to his office?

A: Us prisoners in the jail.

Q: Did he take you all at once, or one at a time?

A: One at a time, him and that other lawyer took us to his office and asked us questions about Lt. Manion.

Q: Were you promised a lighter sentence if you came over here and went on the witness stand?

Q: [Dancer] Your Honor, the people object that this is irrelevant and unfounded.

J: Overruled.

A bad objection which only makes things even worse.

A: I wasn't promised anything.

Q: You just thought it would help your own troubles if you dreamed up this story to please the DA.

A: I didn't dream up nothing.

Q: You're sure that's what Lt. Manion said?

A: Yeah, I'm sure.

Q: Just as sure as you were about your criminal record?

A: Well, I guess I kind of goofed on that one.

Q: Your Honor, I don't feel that I can dignify this creature with any more questions.

Mr. Biegler does well damaging both the witness and the prosecution's credibility given the witness's lack of truthfulness about his criminal record and his claim of getting no benefit from the testimony as well as the prosecutor's fishing for and incentivizing every inmate to provide incriminating information on Lt. Manion.

Now, if this witness had been properly handled on direct examination, rejecting Sammy's Rule and understanding that the problems cannot be ignored, these things would have been dealt with in advance. Instead, the prosecution has once again violated Sammy's Rule and acted like no one could see their problems as long as they kept their own eyes closed.

Lt. Frederick Manion

The defense recalls the defendant, Lieutenant Frederick Manion:

Q: Now, you've heard the testimony of this Miller. Is any part of it true?

A: None.

> Q: Lieutenant, do you have any idea why he might
> come here with a tale like that?
> A: No, sir.

This was very poorly done. The defendant should not have
been recalled and, if so, the answer should have been that
the witness made the story up to get out of trouble after
being incentivized by the prosecution to lie.

> Q: Have you ever talked with this man?
> A: Yes.
> Q: And what did you talk about?
> A: Nothing important. Certainly nothing about my
> personal life or my feelings.

Based on the strong cross-examination of Mr. Miller and
his direct examination, there was simply no reason to have
the defendant testify again. Not only was there no benefit,
but there is a significant negative since he gets cross-examined again.

Claude Dancer cross-examines for the prosecution:

> Q: Lieutenant Manion, have you ever had any sort of
> trouble with Miller?
> A: I don't know, what do you mean, an argument,
> something like that?

Mr. Dancer asks a controlled open-ended question to
see if the witness will answer or play games. The witness
claims not to understand the question and asks a question
back. This is the kind of unforced error that Mr. Dancer's

question was designed to create and now he has to take advantage of it by Pulling the Chain.

> Q: Well, did you ever attack Miller? Physically attack him? Your lawyer can't answer the question for you, lieutenant. Did you ever physically attack Miller?
>
> A: Well, I wouldn't exactly call it an attack. I pushed his head against the bars, one day.

Mr. Dancer was impatient and decided to rephrase into a leading question. But he shouldn't have been in a rush. Instead, he should have made it clear that the witness was playing games.

> Q: Why?
>
> A: He said something ugly about my wife.

Another missed opportunity to Pull the Chain and to diminish the witness's credibility for claiming that pushing another man's head against the metal cell bars was not an attack.

> Q: Do you remember pushing or bumping his head against the bars?
>
> A: Well, sure, I just told you.
>
> Q: Then this was not Dissociative Reaction?
>
> Q: [Biegler] The defendant is not qualified to answer that.
>
> J: Sustained.

Everything has been leading to this point. The witness has damaged his own credibility along the way because he knows this is a problem and has no way of stopping it. Now Mr. Biegler desperately tries to stop it using the only tool he has, an objection. It is successful because Mr. Dancer has used the clinical term, but it will be a hollow victory.

> Q: Lieutenant Manion, wasn't your action against Barney Quill much the same as your action against Miller and against the lieutenant that you struck at the cocktail party? All in the heat of anger, with the conscious desire to hurt or kill?
> A: I don't remember my action against Quill.

A devastating question that puts the entire theory into a neat bow. The only problem is that Mr. Dancer doesn't go further. The best piece of evidence the prosecution has is that the defendant on three occasions attacked other men about his wife and the only time he doesn't remember it and claims no culpability is for this act against Mr. Quill.

> Q: How long had you known your wife was running around with Barney Quill?
> A: I never knew anything like that. I trust my wife.
> Q: I suppose you just beat her up occasionally just for the fun of it.
> Q: [Biegler] Nothing has been established to permit a question like that. He keeps implying things without ever getting to the point. Let him ask the lieutenant, "Did he ever beat his wife?"

J: I'll sustain the objection. Would you like to rephrase your question, Mr. Dancer?

Q: No thank you, your Honor. I'm finished.

Mr. Dancer asked the perfect question, which encapsulated his theory of the case and put the defendant into the very difficult position of having to say that of all the times he attacked other men regarding his wife were different than this one. But Mr. Dancer shouldn't have stopped there, and he shouldn't have journeyed into an area where he didn't have the power to win the argument. Instead, he should have gone further into the line of questioning about attacking others over his wife, going deeply into each incident of violence to buttress the argument that his actions against Mr. Quill were the same as the others.

Finally, when Mr. Dancer made his improper statement and Mr. Biegler objected to it and dared him to ask the question, Mr. Dancer ran away. Doing this is a terrible mistake because it looks like the cross-examiner is afraid of the answer. Mr. Dancer should instead have asked the question and used the two inarguable times he slapped her as proof that he did, in fact, beat his wife. Even more, Mr. Biegler's ill-advised and goading objection actually helps push the prosecution to deal with a material issue that needs to be dealt with. Let's examine how Mr. Dancer could have done better after Mr. Biegler's re-direct.

Biegler re-directs for the defense:

Q: Then I'll ask. Did you, Lieutenant Manion, ever beat your wife, on the night of the shooting or at any other time?

A: No, sir.

Q: Is there any doubt in your mind that Barney Quill raped Mrs. Manion?

A: No, sir.

Lt. Manion was badly damaged on cross-examination, but Mr. Biegler was able to capitalize on Mr. Dancer's failure to finish the cross-examination well. As such, he is able to come back in and look like the credible truth-telling advocate who will ask the questions that the trier of fact needs to decide the case. As we have discussed, credibility is the coin of the realm and that is what this exchange was all about.

Here's an example of how Mr. Dancer could have more effectively dealt with the important issue and also stopped the defense from damaging his credibility:

Q: *Have you ever beaten your wife?*

A: *Well, I've slapped her before, but I've never beaten her up.*

Q: *So slapping her and beating her up are different?*

A: *Yes.*

Q: *When you slapped her so hard in a jealous rage that she almost fell off the veranda you weren't beating her up?*

A: *No.*

Q: *You slapped your wife so hard she almost fell off a veranda because you thought that she encouraged another man to cut in on the dance floor?*

A: *Yes.*

> Q: *Not only did you beat her because you thought she was encouraging him to cut in on the dance floor, but you attacked him, too?*
>
> A: *I did hit him.*
>
> Q: *Given those attacks over a dance floor cut in, what would you do to her and the other man if she actually cheated on you?*

You can surely hear the response in your mind, as would the judge and jury. As we have previously discussed, Mrs. Manion's physical injuries are probably the key issue in determining whether her story is true or not. If Mr. Quill did it, then the jury will likely believe her and conclude that she was raped by him. On the other hand, if it concludes that the defendant did it, then the defense case likely falls apart. Given this paradigm, the prosecution must meet this issue head on. The way to do it is by juxtaposing the defendant's previous jealous conduct over a lesser issue to argue that he probably would kill the other man and severely beat his wife if she cheated on him.

Mary Polan

The defense calls Mary Polan as a rebuttal witness:

> Q: Where do you live, Miss Polan?
>
> A: At the Thunder Bay Inn in Thunder Bay.
>
> Q: And how long have you lived there?
>
> A: For two years.
>
> Q: And what's your profession?
>
> A: I manage the Inn.

Q: Now, Miss Polan, how is the laundry handled at the Thunder Bay Inn?

A: It's chuted down to the laundry room.

Q: And where is the location of that chute on the second floor?

A: Between room 42 and 43.

Q: Who lives in those rooms?

A: I live in 42. Mr. Quill lived in 43.

Q: Now, would Mr. Quill, coming up from the lobby, have to pass by the mouth of that chute on the way to his room?

A: Yes.

Q: Would it be very easy for him to drop something into that chute as he passed by?

A: Yes.

Q: Have you ever had occasion to go down into the laundry at any time?

A: Yes, part of my job is to sort various pieces of laundry as they come out of the wash and dry machines.

Q: Would you tell the court what you found among those pieces of laundry the day after Mr. Quill was killed?

A: I found a pair of women's panties.

Q: And what did you do with them?

A: I threw them into the rag bin.

Q: When did you learn the significance of these panties?

A: Here, this morning, in the courtroom.

Q: And then you went home and got them out of the rag bin?

A: Yes.

Q: Did you bring them with you?

A: Yes.

Q: I offer this article of lingerie as Exhibit #1 for the defense. They're white, they have lace up the side, and they're badly torn as if they've been ripped apart by powerful hands. The label reads, "Smart Shop, Phoenix Arizona."

J: If there's no objection, the exhibit will be received into evidence.

Claude Dancer cross-examines for the prosecution:

Q: Did you ever talk to Mr. Lodwick, the prosecuting attorney, about the death of Barney Quill?

A: Yes, he came to the hotel several times after Mr. Quill was killed.

Q: Did you tell Mr. Lodwick that you didn't believe Barney Quill had raped Mrs. Manion?

A: Yes, I told him that.

Q: Now, Miss Polan, did you ever talk to Mr. Biegler, the defense attorney?

A: Yes.

Q: Was this also in connection with the shooting of Quill?

A: Yes.

Q: Did you tell him that you didn't believe Barney Quill had raped Mrs. Manion?

A: Yes.

Q: How many times did you talk to Mr. Biegler?

A: Twice.

Q: When was the last time?

A: Last night.

Q: And have you changed your mind? Do you now believe Barney Quill raped Mrs. Manion?

A: I don't know now. I think he might have.

Q: When did you change your mind, last night?

A: No, no, it was here this morning.

Q: When were you given the panties, was that last night?

Q: [Biegler] Now wait a minute, just wait a minute—

J: Use the proper form of objection, Mr. Biegler.

Q: [Biegler] No, on second thought, I don't object, your Honor. I want the jury to hear her answer.

Just because we can object, doesn't mean that we should. Mr. Dancer's question is a direct Credibility Attack that claims that the witness and the defense are in a conspiracy to plant evidence. Mr. Biegler shouldn't be afraid of it if he doesn't have a reason to be.

J: The witness may answer.

A: No, I was not given the panties, last night or at any other time. I found them exactly as I said.

Q: Do you know for a fact that Barney Quill dropped the panties down the chute or did you just assume it?

A: I assumed it.

Mr. Dancer hears the witness's strong answer to his Credibility Attack and shifts to the Limiting technique.

Q: Had you thought that perhaps someone else might have put the panties there, someone who wanted them found in the laundry?

A: I hadn't thought of that.

An excellent question using the Hitchhiking technique.

Q: And in the grip of what Mr. Biegler might call irresistible impulse you rushed in here with the panties because you wanted to crucify the character of a dead Barney Quill, isn't that true?

A: Oh no, I thought it was my duty.

Mr. Dancer now uses the information he has gained using the Limiting and Hitchhiking techniques to go back to a Credibility Attack.

Q: Your pride was hurt, wasn't it?

A: I don't know what you mean.

Q: [Biegler] Your Honor, he's trying to confuse the witness. Let him ask her a question she can understand.

J: Yes, Mr. Dancer, I myself would like to know what you're driving at.

Q: Miss Polan, when you found the panties, was your first thought that Barney Quill might have raped Mrs. Manion, or was it that he might have been stepping out with Mrs. Manion?

A: What does he mean? I don't know what he means.

J: Once again, Mr. Dancer, I must ask you to put straight questions to the witness.

Q: Here's a straight question, your Honor. Miss Polan, were you Barney Quill's mistress?

A: No, I was not.

Q: Do you know it's common knowledge in Thunder Bay that you were living with Quill?

A: He was—

Q: Was what, Miss Polan? Barney Quill was what, Miss Polan?

A: Barney Quill was my father.

Q: No more questions, your Honor.

Endgame. Mr. Dancer is a highly skilled cross-examiner who nevertheless just lost the case. But a cross-examiner's technical skill doesn't matter if the evidence doesn't permit your theory to make sense. And that is Mr. Dancer's fatal flaw: he treated this as a Credibility Attack without possessing the tools to be successful. And as we discussed earlier, we must use the tools to win when we engage in a Credibility Attack because someone will survive and someone will not.

Indeed, Mr. Dancer did elicit critical information from this witness: that she doesn't know how the panties got there and that someone else could have planted them. But Mr. Dancer did not understand the limits of what was possible with this witness. Instead, he pressed further and tried to show that this witness was a liar, bent on ruining Mr. Quill's reputation.

But Miss Polan is not a liar and is actually someone pre-disposed to believing that Mr. Quill did nothing wrong because she was his daughter. Thus, this was doomed once Mr. Dancer axiomatically decided to destroy the witness by arguing she was a liar planting evidence or as a jilted paramour. A climactic ending that demonstrates just how easily a cross-examination can turn into a suicide rather than a homicide.

Summary

Anatomy of a Murder is perhaps the most technically masterful trial film available. The cat and mouse between each side is thrilling and the advocates perform at a high level, controlling the witness with open-ended questions and laying traps for each other. It also puts into context almost every principle that we have endeavored to learn here.

This is a difficult case, a game of inches where mistakes count. While Lt. Manion (and the real life defendant) was found not guilty due to temporary insanity,§ I think this case could have gone either way depending on the quality of the advocates.

---

§   On July 31, 1952 in Big Bay, Michigan, Lt. Coleman A. Peterson shot and killed the Lumberjack Tavern owner Maurice K. Chenowith after Charlotte Peterson claimed that he sexually assaulted her. Charlotte Petersen testified that she was drinking and playing shuffleboard at the tavern and that Mr. Chenowith sexually assaulted her in the woods after offering to drive her home. Lt. Peterson then took a nine-millimeter Luger revolver to the tavern and fired every available round into Mr. Chenowith. A subsequent medical test could not confirm whether she had been assaulted. After being charged with First Degree Murder, Lt. Peterson retained John D. Voelker, who argued that the defendant's act was an "irresistible impulse" resulting from the attack against his wife. This temporary insanity defense relied upon *People vs. Durfee*, 62 Mich. 487 (1886) (which was subsequently over-turned after the Michigan Legislature enacted 1975 PA 1980).

Those interested in learning more about the similarities and differences between the real and fictional cases can review some of the publicly available trial transcripts, as well as an interview with one of the jurors, here: https://nmu.edu/voelker/court_transcripts.htm.

What if the prosecution had accepted that the rape allegation was coming into the case instead of fighting it? What if the prosecution didn't try to prove that Mrs. Manion wasn't raped, but instead claimed that Lt. Manion didn't believe her? What if the prosecution correctly understood the irresistible impulse law? What if the prosecution's expert performed an in-person examination and reached the same conclusion? What if the prosecution's expert was strong in his opinion regardless of whether or not he performed an in-person examination? What if Mr. Dancer didn't try and make Miss Polan a liar? And so on . . .

But that is what makes this case and cross-examination so interesting and important. It is a process of finding the best version of the truth about things that happened in the past and where there is no definitive answer. And the better we all are at cross-examination, the closer we get to the truth.

CHAPTER TWENTY-ONE
The End of the Beginning

So, where do we go from here? My advice is not to treat this as the end of your learning, but instead the end of the beginning. This book has endeavored to provide guidance and direction about cross-examination in a world where there is both too little of it and where what we have is sometimes insufficient.

This book intended to provide the foundation of your process, but it cannot be an end unto itself. There never is an end as long as you continue working on these skills. No one can do that for you. You can, of course, simply decide that reading the book is enough. However, what you will find in this (and most things in life) is that things get even more interesting the deeper you go.

For those who wish to continue forward, my advice is to go back to the beginning of this book and re-read it again. Everything will have enhanced meaning because it is not possible to fully grasp all of this on one read-through. The next step is to get up on your feet. It doesn't matter if that is in a class, an in-house mock trial, or in a courtroom over the smallest of controversy. There is only so much thought exercise that a person can do until it is time to feel the actual sensation of flight. Nothing can take the place of actual experience. But as I have written, experience without thoughtful analysis is simply not good enough.

A final thought: the title of this work is *The Absolute Beginner's Guide to Cross-Examination*, but that is a misnomer. This book is not just for beginners. That would have been an impossibility for me. I only know one way to teach these principles and that is all the way. It is rather a book to make a beginning upon, growing in thinking and experience, and ultimately adding your own insights.

After all, that's what I did with the teachings of those who came before me . . .

Endnotes

1. Fred Ebb and John Kander, "Razzle Dazzle" (Recorded by Jerry Orbach and the Original Broadway Cast), *Chicago* (1975), https://www.allmusicals.com/lyrics/chicago/razzledazzle.htm.
2. *White Men Can't Jump*, directed by Ron Shelton (20th Century Fox, 1992).
3. *Mad Max Beyond Thunderdome*, directed by George Miller and George Ogilvie (Warner Brothers, 1985).
4. *My Cousin Vinny*, directed by Jonathan Lynn (20th Century Fox, 1992). All quotations within Chapter 18 are from the same source, unless otherwise noted.
5. *White Men Can't Jump*, directed by Ron Shelton (20th Century Fox, 1992).
6. *A Few Good Men*, directed by Rob Reiner (Columbia Pictures, 1992). All quotes from Chapter Nineteen are from the same source, unless otherwise noted.
7. *Anatomy of a Murder*, directed by Otto Preminger (Columbia Pictures, 1959). All quotes from Chapter Twenty are from the same source, unless otherwise noted.

Index

NOTES

NOTES

NOTES

NOTES

NOTES

NOTES

NOTES

NOTES

NOTES

NOTES

NOTES

NOTES

NOTES

NOTES